G000279218

Finding God in Brazil

Finding God in Brazil

Personal stories to amaze and inspire

Dr John B Dyer

Registered with the IP Rights Office
Copyright Registration Service
Ref: 9504643110

First published 2017

Second edition, with revisions, May 2018

Third edition, November 2018

Map of Brazil by One Stop Map/<u>onestopmap.com</u>

Prologue

Many of the stories that unfold in this book are known only to me and my wife, Maria. Of course, the participants involved in each story may well remember these moments with fondness, laughter or anguish, and perhaps a mixture of all three. But it occurred to me that the full story of our time in Brazil is known only to two people and the chief protagonist, our wonderful God, who made this story possible. The story and stories are being told here, with the desire to make known the mystery and wonder of his ways, in his dealings with ordinary human beings.

While I was researching for my doctoral studies on grassroots theological education in Brazil, a missionary colleague recommended a book by John Burdick. It goes by the title: *Looking for God in Brazil.* The book is about the progressive Catholic Church and explains how the radical wing of the church in Brazil was lagging behind the explosive growth of Pentecostalism and Afro-Brazilian Spiritism. The title of Burdick's book points to a quest to find God in urban Brazil, particularly in the city of Rio de Janeiro. The present story, *Finding God in Brazil,* describes encounters with God in unexpected places on the part of the people we met across that vast country; their hopes and fears, as well as our own. God is there for us when we need him; in situations beyond our control and also those of our own making.

Some of the material used in these stories has been retrieved from our personal archives stored away for many years. To be truthful, even I had forgotten some of the details, and had to be reminded from the letters we wrote about events at the time; a reminder to us of the Gospels, which all those years ago, were written before the first-hand witnesses had passed from the scene. The passage of time and forgetfulness was another of the reasons that we felt we should write these things down now so that a permanent record existed when we were no longer here to tell the story ourselves.

And so, our story begins.

My wife, Maria, and I both grew up in the London area. We worked in London, she in a well-known Bank. My own work experience was for the State Government of Victoria, Australia at their office in the Strand. At the age of eighteen, I made my public profession of faith in Jesus Christ and was baptised by immersion at the local Baptist church in Holmesdale Road, South Norwood.

My call to the ministry was not a Damascus Road experience, as in the case of the apostle Paul. I had other ideas about my future work and was planning to obtain professional qualifications in business and marketing. There was, however, an inaudible still, small voice at the back of my mind that prompted me from time to time. This was more akin to the experience of the prophet Elijah than the apostle

Paul. Eventually, I decided to test the waters, and I applied to Spurgeon's College in South London. Spurgeon's College is a theological college for the training of Baptist ministers, founded by the Victorian preacher, Charles Haddon Spurgeon in 1856. Spurgeon's College was only a short distance from where I lived with my family until my teens.

My application to the college to train as a Baptist minister was successful, and this was the beginning of a massive shift in the direction of my life. To begin with, I had no thoughts about living or working abroad. However, by the end of my second year of study, I sensed that I should be thinking about service overseas. This was the first time that such a thought had occurred to me. Looking back, I believe the thought process would have started when I heard a Baptist missionary from my home church at Holmesdale Road, South Norwood, speak about her work as a nursing sister in the Belgian Congo, as it was known then. She spoke about her experiences as a missionary in a vivid and colourful way, and she held my attention throughout her talk.

So, I made an appointment to visit the headquarters of the Baptist Missionary Society (BMS), at Gloucester Place, in Central London. The instruction I received from that visit was to return during my final year at college when I would be in a position to make a formal offer of service.

My focus for the next two years was to conclude my theological studies and pray about the future. I was already quite set on the idea of being a missionary in Africa. The two years passed, and I was back at BMS in London to discuss the next step.

Sitting across the table was the kindly figure of the Reverend Fred Drake, the Overseas Secretary. He seemed hesitant to start the conversation. The first question he asked me was: 'Do you have an open mind as to where overseas God might want you to serve?' I knew that the right answer to that question should be - Yes. At the same time, I was sure in my heart that it was to serve in the Congo. So, I answered, 'Yes.' That was as far as we got discussing the Congo, as the discussion was then guided towards Brazil. After our meeting, I must admit I felt devastated. I now had to begin to take from my mind all that I had thought about over the previous two years. Did I want to go to Brazil? I really didn't know.

At the College, one of my contemporaries was João Garcia, a Brazilian student on a BMS scholarship. One day soon after my interview at BMS, he and I were walking along the main street in Upper Norwood. He began to share with me the challenge of pastoral and evangelistic work Brazil; in particular, he mentioned the new government initiative to open up the interior of the country by building a road from east to west. This was to be known as the Trans-Amazonian Highway, and new towns would be established at forty-five-mile intervals along this new highway. The thought of perhaps being involved in this drew me like a magnet. The more I thought about it, the more I liked the idea. Brazil, it was!

I had already met Maria through a church Holiday Club at her home church in South East London. I helped lead that Club during my first summer vacation in 1969. It wasn't until the young people's Easter Bible Class Camp in Southampton, in 1971 that we started going out. We became engaged in 1973 and married at the beginning of May the following year.

We didn't get to Brazil overnight. In fact, it was another six years before that became a reality. To gain experience of pastoral ministry, I first worked alongside Alan Easter, the minister of a large Baptist church in Ipswich, Suffolk. I followed that with a pastorate in the city centre of Birmingham.

Impatient though I was to get to Brazil, I was able to complete the requirements for ministerial recognition with the Baptist Union. The experience of ministry in these two churches was to serve me well, even more than I could have imagined at the time. On arriving in Brazil, every bit of my experience would be needed.

Walking along the Trans-Amazonian Highway

The time was getting closer for our journey to Brazil, and we were both keen to get going. It was a major adventure in a land as yet unknown. We would be living in a country with an unfamiliar language, and a culture very different from the British way of life.

Just as we were about to leave for Brazil, there came an unexpected delay. The Brazilian Government had decided to stop issuing visas for missionaries.

Up to that time visas had been relatively easy to obtain. Apparently, certain people had decided to apply for visas under the pretence of being missionaries, but they were not. The weeks of waiting turned into months. Six months passed and still, no new visas for missionaries were issued by Brasilia. We decided to try other avenues of service. We had left our church in Birmingham and finished missionary training at Selly Oak College. As mentioned before, at the start of my working life, I had worked for the Australian Government in the Strand, London. I had always had a fascination for Australia from geography lessons at school and from boyhood memories of Australian peaches for dessert at Sunday lunch. I decided to apply to the Baptist Union of South Australia for a possible posting to a church in that state. The idea was reinforced when the General Secretary of that organisation, who was in London at the time, invited us to meet him for

Trans-Amazonian Highway

breakfast one morning. This meeting led to an exchange of correspondence including a statement from us concerning our ministerial vision and theological stance.

The outcome was encouraging, and we were informed that the churches in South Australia would be interested in inviting a couple like ourselves to work alongside them. We were eager to proceed.

Then there came another letter from the General Secretary with one final question before placing our name before the churches in South Australia. The problem was this: 'If we were to receive our visas from the Brazilian Government, would we terminate our interest in going to Australia?'

How does one answer that kind of question? We knew we had to give an honest answer, and that we would have to abide by our decision. Above all, we wanted to do God's will. But how could we know whether God wanted us in Brazil or Australia?

To obtain the answer to that question, we decided to ask BMS if they would allow us to go to the Brazilian Consulate and clarify the situation relating to our visa application. Typically, BMS would not agree to this, as they like to handle all negotiations relating to visas themselves; however, on this occasion, they gave us permission to approach the Consulate directly. Our position was as follows: my wife and I had decided that if our visas were not yet in London, we would go to Australia. If they were, we would go to Brazil.

We arrived at the Brazilian Consulate in London the day after the Spring Bank Holiday 1978. As we made our way up to the visa department, we knew we had come to a watershed moment in our lives. There is a big difference between going to Brazil, and all that country would demand from us, and going to Australia, an English-speaking country on the other side of the world. But it was one or the other, and we would soon know the answer.

We walked into the room and approached the desk; that very day we would discover our destiny. We had decided the simple formula that would determine where we were going. Even before we spoke, she said: 'I've got something for you.' How she knew who we were and what we wanted, we never knew. To our astonishment, our visas had been granted the previous day which was a Bank Holiday in England. They had been faxed through from Brasilia and were available for us at the Consulate. If we had gone to the Consulate on the Friday before the Bank Holiday instead of the Tuesday following, we would have gone to Australia. As it happened, we were on our way to Brazil.

Since that day, we have always felt that God called us twice to Brazil. And that conviction has kept us on track in Brazil for more than three decades. When the going got tough in later years, we have been able to refer back to that exact moment. When we were told that our visas had arrived, it was a miraculous moment. There was such a moment around five years later, at the end of September 1983. We received the devastating news that we had lost our first child, a baby daughter. She had died in the womb just one month short of full term. Our return to Brazil had been postponed so that Maria could give birth in London, in the hospital where she herself had been born. The devastation we experienced caused us to contemplate remaining in England. But again, we needed to know what God wanted. We received from well-meaning friends, words of comfort and advice. The problem was that the advice pointed us in two opposite directions; to remain in England, but also to return to Brazil (in one case without delay). The leadership of our local church in South East London was made up of elders and deacons. We asked the pastor to help us resolve our dilemma. Our personal choice was to stay in England and not to return to Brazil. We still had much grieving to do, and the thought of not being able to visit our daughter's grave was daunting. In a strange way, we felt that there, we could be together. We knew in our hearts, though, that she had gone to heaven to be one of God's angels.

The elders of the church met together at their weekly meeting. The pastor had already told us that he was sure that they would recommend we remain in England. We had arranged to phone him after their meeting, as we were away from home on a short break. There were no mobiles in those days, so we could only communicate via a public phone box in the village of Acol, in Kent.

We made the call hoping the answer would be to remain in England. We were told that when the elders met, they had each sensed that we should not return to Brazil. Then they prayed, and God spoke to each one of them. Surprisingly, after they had prayed, they knew that we should return to Brazil, as soon as possible. The answer I received on the phone in Acol went against our own immediate feelings and desires.

Our return to Brazil was delayed due to a miscarriage in February 1984; however, our resolve was intact, and that was to follow God's leading as we believed it had been given to us by the church elders. Shortly after, I was at a retreat for BMS missionaries at High Leigh in Hertfordshire. Maria was still recovering from the miscarriage, both physically and emotionally, but encouraged me to go. It was there that our good friend Reginald Harvey, the BMS General Director, urged us to return to Brazil as soon as we could. That, he said, was in our own best interests. We were once again focused on the future. On 10th June 1984, we boarded our plane at Heathrow Airport, still tearful but with the knowledge that we were safe in God's keeping and at the centre of his will.

In the following pages, we recount this and other deeply significant experiences. We travel to places far off the beaten track; places where the tourists never set foot. This story is about a fascinating country and its extraordinary people. The experiences that we are about to share with you have sometimes given us deep anguish, but also exhilarating joy. The Brazil we know best is the Brazil we have rubbed shoulders with for over 30 years. These are also the stories of those we were privileged to serve in Christ's name. Before we could meet and greet new friends in a far-off land, we had to go through all the emotional processes connected with a tearful farewell. We were leaving behind family and friends with all that entailed. We were told that they would feel the separation far more than we would. And, because our lives would be full of so many new things, their sacrifice would inevitably be the more significant.

Over the years, I have come to realise the truth of that statement, especially when our own son left home to go to boarding school in the United Kingdom at the age of sixteen. It was a great bonus that we were able to travel on that first journey to Brazil (and Maria's first in a plane) with our friends and colleagues, Mike and Gill Wotton and their three children, Kathy, Derek and Susie. They knew the ropes, and this was their third trip to Brazil. It was in August 1978 that our British Caledonian Airways plane accelerated down the runway at London's Gatwick Airport. Our new future had begun!

Chapter One

Beginnings

The next day, 23rd August 1978, we touched down in the northeastern Brazilian city of Recife. It was four in the morning, still dark and raining. Our Boeing 707 had already made one stop to refuel in Lisbon. We felt great excitement as we had crossed the Atlantic Ocean and travelled to the southern side of the equator. We took off again in the dark an hour later, on the last leg of our journey to Rio de Janeiro. Within minutes of taking off, dawn broke to the first deep hues of an indigo-violet sky.

This leg of our flight to Rio took three hours. Once on the ground, we had to go through immigration control and, as we were entering the country with permanent residents' visas, it was necessary to present our chest x-rays. These had been taken in London prior to our departure from the United Kingdom.

Although we had done a crash course in Portuguese, we could only assume that the official from the Department of Health at Rio International Airport was asking for a gratuity for his services. We played the dumb foreigner, and eventually, he gave up and allowed us to go. As a result of the delays in immigration, we only just managed to catch our connecting flight to Curitiba, the capital city of the southern state of Paraná.

Land of Contrasts

Our first impression of Brazil, as we drove along the airport road on a cloudy Wednesday morning in August, was that it wasn't so different after all. To be honest, we had expected an entirely different world. Perhaps we had over prepared for the expected culture shock. Apart from the billboards in Portuguese along the way, and the fact that we were driving on the right-hand side of the road, everything looked normal. This impression was reinforced the next day. As we walked down the main street of Curitiba, we were enveloped by the strains of a popular song, which was high in the British charts at the time. The music was coming from a local music shop. Curitiba, so we soon discovered, is a cosmopolitan city, with a strong European influence. Despite the fact that everyone around us was speaking in a language we did not understand, we felt at home. Furthermore, Curitiba was about the size of Birmingham, where we had lived before going to Brazil. What did strike us was the sight of people begging for money on several street corners. However, the real culture shock was two years away, when we returned to the United Kingdom for the first time. By that time, we had been to some very different places in Brazil.

As time passed, we got to know Brazil better. We travelled extensively by road and air and wrote home 15 months later. These were our thoughts at that time:

We have seen the fabulous sights of Rio de Janeiro and the sufferings and poverty of the interior of this vast country of unbelievable contrasts. Hope and despair, optimism and resignation, joy and sadness exist side by side. The one seems oblivious to the other. To this bewildering and contradictory world, we seek to bring a sympathy and love that speaks of God's concern for us all.

On our first Saturday in Brazil, we were invited by our missionary colleagues Brunton Scott and Avelino Ferreira to go with them, and their wives, on a visit to the coastal plain or littoral. We drove down through the mountains, towards the sea, and arrived in Antonina at lunchtime. We stopped by a jetty by the water's edge for a picnic, and to rest before the second part of our journey that afternoon. After about a twenty-minute drive, we left the asphalt and entered what I thought was someone's private land. The dirt track ahead of us was, in fact, the only road leading to the surrounding villages. The following is from our first newsletter home, written a few days later, in September 1978. It describes our feelings about that journey:

We were quite obviously in a new and fascinating world. The climate in that part of Paraná is sub-tropical, unlike the temperate zone of Curitiba. All around were palm trees, sugar cane, banana trees and 'Busy Lizzies' in a profusion of colour. But it is equally true that the lifestyle of some of the people of this area is not quite what we in Britain and many in Brazil are accustomed to. The simple wooden shacks, with oil or gas lighting, were home to many along the road. Their general living conditions are so basic it is hard to imagine how they cope.

We soon learned that this Brazil was worlds apart from anything we had known before. Not that this deterred us; on the contrary, it was the kind of challenge we had hoped for, and one to which we responded with heart and soul.

Initially, we lived near the city centre of Curitiba in an apartment owned by our Mission. The day following our trip to the littoral, we went to church for the first time in Brazil. It was quite unlike anything we had expected or been told about.

We described it at the time as follows:

It is quite a small fellowship, and the members are of Slavic stock. They are very friendly and immediately made us feel at home amongst them. In the church garden, there is an orange tree, a lemon tree and a peach tree, all bearing fruit.

There were Bible texts around the walls of the church building written in the congregation's native tongue. The music was also different from what we expected with the traditional mandolin as an accompaniment to the singing of hymns. Today, the church garden is the car park for a new church, led by our friend and colleague, Pastor Jairo. You will meet him later in our story.

Subsequent generations of the original Slavic church families, who had migrated to Brazil for economic reasons in the late 20th century, or who had fled Soviet persecution in the mid-20th century, had little interest in perpetuating the mother tongue of the original settlers. The church is now a Brazilian church, with a brand-new building and a very different congregation. The reminders of its past are now kept safely in a separate room.

Our first house
We soon found a little house to set up as our home. It was a small detached bungalow, on the eastern outskirts of Curitiba. The following is how we described our new home to friends and family in England:

> In a few days, we are to move into a house at Capão da Imbuia, a suburb of Curitiba. The house is just right for us. It is made of brick (unlike many homes in Brazil which are made of wood) and has a sala (living room), bedroom, study (or 2nd bedroom), kitchen and bathroom. Like most houses in Brazil, it has no upstairs – just like what is known as a bungalow in the United Kingdom.

The house was on a corner plot at the intersection of two dirt roads. It had a garden around three sides, with a lovely yellow flowering tree and huge white lilies, known locally as *copo de leite* or 'milk cup.'

It was exciting finding out about our new Brazilian neighbourhood and beginning formal language study at the Baptist seminary. This was on the other side of town. Portuguese is a beautiful Latin-based language. Being phonetic makes pronouncing Portuguese words relatively easy, but the many grammatical rules that have to be applied can make learning the language hard going. Thankfully, our teachers did a good job, and we are grateful to them for their patience and dedication throughout that first year in Brazil. As you will discover by reading on, learning a new language was accomplished not only in the classroom but also on the job. Sometimes our attempts to speak in Portuguese led to misunderstandings which often produced hilarious results. One morning after language study, I was talking with one of the female secretaries at the Baptist seminary. She asked me a question about the British Royal Family, and I informed her that I had seen the Queen in the flesh. Astonishment was written all over her face. Apparently, the expression 'in the flesh' is understood by Brazilians as 'without any clothes.'

Bethel Baptist Church

During our first year in Brazil, we were under the pastoral care of the Bethel Baptist Church down the road from where we lived. The pastor, Samuel Lagos Mallo, his wife and family, and, indeed, the whole church, were so welcoming and helpful. Within a couple of months, I was given the opportunity to preach my first sermon in Portuguese (written word for word), and I must say the congregation was extraordinarily kind and generous in its appreciation. Brazil was known then, certainly, as the land of tomorrow. It was an exciting place to be; always a building project underway, on a piece of land nearby, and with three-quarters of the population under 25 years of age, it was a vibrant, forward-looking nation. And still is.

Our first tour

The next step for us also involved looking to the future. By the beginning of 1979, we were being guided by our Mission towards our location where we would eventually work following our language study in Curitiba. First thoughts were that we could go to the neighbouring state of Santa Catarina to the south. Following a short holiday with missionary colleagues at a Baptist retreat centre on the coast of Santa Catarina, it had been arranged for us to do a reconnaissance tour of the eastern region of that state. The following is taken from our written reflections immediately after that tour. This account will give you a feel for the dynamics of Brazilian Baptist life:

Following a briefing by Pastor Almir Etelvino Santos, Executive Secretary of the Santa

Catarina Baptist Convention on the morning of 10 January, we began our tour the next day. We set out from the state capital city of Florianópolis, where we had stayed overnight enjoying excellent hospitality in the home of North American missionaries, Bill Moseley and his wife. It was there that we sampled iced tea for the first time. At the suggestion of Pastor Almir, we first visited the coastal resort of Camboriú, and then the adjoining town of Itajaí. The situation in the church at Itajaí was an unhappy one. During the four years ministry of the pastor, the relationship between him and his congregation had become strained. The pastor was due to leave the church at the end of January.

Four years previously, the Itajaí church had a membership of eighty. It had now dwindled to fourteen. The church had commenced a new building project, but, owing to a shortage of money in the latter stages, this remained unfinished at the time of our visit.

According to Pastor Almir, the church was not in a position to support a new pastor and might well be interested in having a missionary. To date there had been no request from the church for help; however, Pastor Almir anticipated that this would come shortly.

We were able to see the new church building, and although there was still work to be done on it, it was being used for worship. It enjoyed an excellent position close to the centre of town. From enquiries we made, it seemed that people in the area knew its location.

The Itajaí church was responsible for the congregation at Camboriú, situated on the further side of the BR 101 highway which linked Curitiba and Florianópolis. Here we found a goodly sized community presenting the church leadership with a genuine challenge in terms of outreach and evangelism. The sanctuary was well cared for and in a good position relative to housing and the population generally.

At the time Itajaí had a population of 100,000 people. It has a fishing industry and is a seaport for ocean-going vessels. Unfortunately, Baptist work there had suffered as a result of the difficulties already mentioned. The church needed to take full advantage of the possibilities for outreach and church growth but appeared unable to do so without substantial help, both financial and pastoral. Maria and I felt drawn to this situation, and Pastor Almir suggested that we might visit there again in February to meet church folk. We then moved on further north to Joinville, the largest city in Santa Catarina, where we spent the night in a very comfortable hotel. Joinville has enjoyed a marked German influence over the years, as can be seen from its architecture; however, the name of the town is French. The next morning (12 Jan) we made a brief visit to the pastor of the Joinville church. We found him to be friendly and helpful. He mentioned that if we were to do orientation in Joinville, he would do all he could to assist us.

The next stop on our tour was Jaraguá do Sul which is an inland industrial town with a population of 42,000. We stopped for lunch and then visited the local church. We then went to the house of one of the church leaders (although only to collect him and a student from Rio de Janeiro who was taking part in the Trans-Catarinense Operation, this was a state-wide evangelistic initiative). From his house, we went to the church. Although we had been impressed with the town of Jaraguá do Sul, we felt disappointment about the location of the church. There was a plan in place to build another sanctuary, but this was scheduled for a site immediately adjacent to the existing building. Apparently, the cost of purchasing a site nearer to the centre of town was prohibitive. The student whom we met commented that it was difficult explaining to people he visited how to get to the church as the route was a bit complicated.

Interestingly, though, about twenty children and the same number of adults had been attending the different meetings arranged for that particular week of outreach.

From Jaraguá do Sul, we moved northwards to Corupá. We found this to be a charming town, and the Baptist church well situated on the main road out to the manufacturing town of São Bento do Sul.

São Bento do Sul has a thriving furniture industry and a population of 30,000. The journey there took us through some spectacular mountain scenery along a gravel road. We felt that the designated site for a church building on the outskirts of the town would become more strategic as that side of town grew and expanded. We did not feel that the location would serve São Bento itself, but would be useful for a more localised operation. We did appreciate the genuine opportunity for a church there as a new housing development was in progress.

We continued westwards to Mafra, following the river Negro that divides Santa Catarina and Paraná states. We then moved southwards and eastwards to our next destination in Rio do Sul in the central valley of the river Itajaí-Açu. In all, we spent 42 hours in Rio do Sul (Friday evening – Sunday midday). This was sufficient time to form impressions of the many possibilities for a church there.

It was here that we met a team of students from Rio de Janeiro and a Brazilian national missionary from the state of Espírito Santo. Like the student we had met previously in Jaraguá do Sul, they too were sharing in the Trans-Catarinense Operation. They told us that they were getting six or seven children at the afternoon meeting for youngsters, and, at the evening service, there were two families and one other gentleman who was a Mennonite.

One of the two families was José, his wife and mother-in-law and children. We were very impressed with his credentials as a church leader, and also by the initiative which had come from him for a Baptist work to be started in Rio do Sul. Incidentally, a house is now being rented close to the town centre (with American Southern Baptist funds), and it is here that the church is officially situated. The church was officially inaugurated in mid-December. There is also the possibility of the church buying time from the local radio station, and this was under consideration at the time of our visit.

We were both very interested to see what was being attempted there and I was glad of the opportunity to give my testimony on the Saturday evening. On the Sunday morning, I preached from John's Gospel, chapter 20:19-22 & 26-31 about some characteristics of the New Testament Church. I applied what I was saying to the church in Rio do Sul, albeit with the help of Bill Moseley (our American companion on this tour) interpreting.

During the afternoon we continued on our way as far as Blumenau. Here we had the opportunity to visit the Baptist church, where I preached at the evening service on the theme 'Ambassadors for Christ' from 2 Corinthians 5:20. The church at Blumenau was seeking a Brazilian pastor, having been without one for around three years. We felt a great sense of privilege in having been invited to make this tour and learned much from it. We were especially grateful to Pastor Almir and Bill Moseley for their help and encouragement.

We felt that it would be a good idea to return to Itajaí again, to meet with the church leaders and others there, before making any decisions concerning the possibility of our working in any of the situations we saw during the tour.

Altogether, we covered six-hundred-and-fifty-six miles during those four days. The irony was that at the very time we were doing this tour in the state of Santa Catarina, our good friend Fred Drake, the Baptist Missionary Society Overseas Secretary, was visiting the northwest of Brazil. Unbeknown to us he was coming to some very different conclusions about our future work in that country.

Chapter Two

On our own

It was with some trepidation that we waved goodbye to our senior missionary colleague. As his plane sped down the airport runway in the northwestern territory of Rondônia, I realised there was no going back now. Our colleague was returning home to the relative comforts of the capital city of the neighbouring state of Mato Grosso. Maria and I looked at each other and wondered what lay in store for us. Two people raised and educated in the relative affluence of the United Kingdom, and now about to begin life in the Amazon rainforest.

One major positive was that Rondônia was about to become the 'new star in the Union' and be transformed from a territory to statehood. A brief word of explanation here: the Brazilian national flag features a number of stars each representing a state of the federation on a blue globe. So Rondônia was about to become the 'new star.' The new state was now to be administered from Porto Velho a city situated on the banks of the River Madeira, a major tributary of the mighty Amazon. This change in status gave the new state the potential to receive a major impetus for its future development. The name was given to the region in memory of an army engineer, Cândido Rondon, who, despite considerable difficulties, was able to extend the telecommunications system into the northwest of Brazil, in the late 19th and early 20th centuries. It was nearly a century later before the next significant advance for telecommunications in the interior of the new state. This next step forward came when the 1982 World Cup was held in Spain. Until then, the territory had no direct TV signal to or from the rest of the country, and the evening national news programmes, broadcast from Rio de Janeiro, were recorded on tapes and sent to the local TV station to be shown the following evening. Now we could receive live coverage of programmes, not only from other parts of Brazil but also from Europe and the rest of the world.

Arriving in the Amazon, a new life unfolded for us. It was full of surprises, some pleasant and others definitely less so. Our Portuguese was still quite rudimentary but was sufficient to make ourselves understood. We soon discovered that language and communication have four parts: listening, speaking, reading and writing. Reading was the easiest and listening with understanding the hardest. We made our mistakes, of course, some quite hilarious, which at least made the Brazilians laugh: some words in Portuguese are very similar, such as *jóias* (meaning 'jewels') and *joelhos* (meaning 'knees'). So, one day, when we were entertaining some young people at our home in Porto Velho, we showed them some pictures of London, including the Tower of London. Trying to sound very knowledgeable, we explained that the Queen's knees were kept in the Tower because of their priceless worth!

A dangerous reptile

Now from the hilarious to the scary: we had been in Rondônia for only a few weeks and, while looking for a permanent place to live in town, were staying at the Wycliffe Bible Translators Base, in the surrounding forest. At night we had the company of bats in the roof. One day, Maria approached the washing line on our veranda and saw that something was different about it. As she walked under it, she looked up, and there was a snake looking straight down at her. We called for help, and several men came armed with machetes. Unfortunately (from our point of view), the snake got away and 'snaked' off under the house. This didn't entirely resolve the matter, as far as we were concerned. We were offered the use of another house, snake and bat free, which we gladly accepted.

When we moved into the town of Porto Velho a few weeks later, we discovered a tarantula at the front garden gate. It had been raining so the ground was muddy. To deal with this unwelcome spider so near the house, I got a bottle and pressed the poor creature into the mud until it no longer presented any danger to human life. One evening, returning from church in Vilhena, where we spent our final two years in Rondônia, we encountered a huge rat behind the curtain in the lounge. I tried hitting it with a broom but to no avail. It just ran through the living room, into the kitchen and then on to the veranda at the back of the house. We were told that only the largest rat trap would be capable of dealing with this kind of rodent. Even then, the trap would have to be securely tied to something solid or heavy to stop the rat running off with its neck in the trap. We tied the trap to our bike which was leaning against the wooden partition wall between the main bedroom and the veranda outside. Having duly armed the trap and tied it to the bike, we went to bed and waited. Not long after, the bike began to rattle against the partition. It seemed to go on for ages until eventually, all was still and quiet. I went out to the veranda; untying the trap, I picked it and the rat up and took both into the garden. I dug a hole, released the rat from the trap, dropping it into the hole. Finally, I poured in a large quantity of kerosene. With the use of a single match the problem was resolved. The snake got away, the bats remained, but the rat and the tarantula were outwitted and disposed of safely. Something that really surprised us while on the Wycliffe Base was the sounds of the forest at night. The jungle comes to life at sunset with the sounds of crickets, frogs and a myriad of other insects. Amazon country is both fascinating and haunting. It beckons to be explored and yet, for the most part, remains impenetrable. We arrived in Porto Velho in September, the beginning of the rainy season.

Roads and Rivers

There were no paved roads out of town, except for the first few miles; so, travel was precarious and challenging, if not virtually impossible at times. This added to the sense of isolation. Distances between towns and other centres of civilisation and the weather meant that for six months of the year travel could only be done by plane. Some of the smaller rivers and streams were bridged by huge logs, the width apart of lorry wheels. Crossing these, required great accuracy, as a deviation to the right or left would have left us and our mini jeep in the river. The logging that was commonplace in the Amazon meant that wider lorries carrying colossal tree logs from the forest, made deep channels in the dirt roads, far too deep for a family saloon car to pass safely. To negotiate these conditions required dexterity of hand at the steering wheel. In a newsletter, written home in May 1979, we described the situation:

On the Trans-Amazonian Highway crossing the Madeira River

The principal highway between Porto Velho and Cuiabá (state of Mato Grosso) is so appalling; it is an act of sheer recklessness to drive a family car (as we did!), any distance along it.

The art of driving in these conditions is to drive with the front and rear wheels on one side of the car on the high middle bank and the corresponding wheels on the other side of the car in one of the two ruts caused by the weight of heavy vehicles.

On our first exploratory journey to the interior of Rondônia, we managed to sheer off the exhaust pipe of the car we had borrowed from a Brazilian pastor in Porto Velho. This was all the more embarrassing because I was driving at the time, and two of the passengers were our Mission's Regional Secretary and the Executive Director of the Baptist Convention of Rondônia and the adjoining state of Acre. It was a steep learning curve, and a mistake I never made again. This unfortunate and quite unforgettable incident happened during our initial reconnaissance tour of the region, a few months before we actually moved there the following September.

Rondônia was still awaiting its emancipation as a state and was being administered from Brasilia, the national capital. In the late seventies and early eighties, there were three Brazilian territories, including Rondônia. The other two were Roraima in the extreme north, the last swathe of Brazilian territory before Venezuela. The third territory was Amapá at the mouth of the River Amazon. All have long since become fully fledged states.

We described our experience of this exploratory journey in a letter to our parents in the United Kingdom, of which a draft copy was found in our apartment in Curitiba during a two-month stay in

2017. The following conveys our first-hand impressions of this remote and largely unknown part of Brazil:

We did the trip to the north of Brazil during the middle of May (11-21). We set out from Curitiba on the Friday at 7:30 in the morning. We took an ordinary coach to São Paulo, (a seven-hour journey), an incredibly busy city and certainly not a place to relax in. From São Paulo, we caught the overnight coach (with reclining seats, blanket and pillow, free coke, too!). This stage of the journey to Cuiabá takes 24 hours! It's a long time to be travelling, but we were able to sleep quite well during the night, which was a help. We stayed overnight (Saturday 12th) in Cuiabá, at a hotel with air conditioning and on the Sunday morning caught the 10:15 plane to Porto Velho, a one-and-a-half-hour journey. So, we arrived at our destination at mid-day, not too far from the equator, and a winter temperature of 28ºC (83ºF). On the Monday, we began our tour in the direction of Vilhena, a town, 440 miles to the south, along a dirt road with blinding dust, ruts and holes that could easily prove to be the write-off of any saloon car driven without absolute care along its forbidding track. We travelled for two days through the rainforest, where every so often, we would find along the dusty roads some small town, right out of a Wild West film. It was a fascinating journey, like being transported back in time to a period long since forgotten.

There are three principal towns in Rondônia: Porto Velho, Ji-Paraná and Vilhena, equal distances apart. There are others, too, where the forest is being pushed back to make room for the invasion of civilisation. We spent a day in Vilhena – arriving at 7:20 Tuesday evening and leaving at 6:00, Thursday morning. Vilhena has a good climate (warm days and cool evenings) and a population of 5,000. It is well planned with wide streets, a post office, telephone exchange, two schools, a modest hotel, with another under construction, garages and car mechanics (most useful) and an airstrip. We were glad to try out our Portuguese on three occasions at church services during the tour and seem to be making a good impression, which is encouraging.

We set about the return journey to Porto Velho, and then by plane to Cuiabá, where we booked a hotel room for a few hours, before taking the overnight coach for the long haul back to São Paulo and Curitiba. We left Cuiabá at 7:30 on Saturday evening and arrived in Curitiba on Monday morning at 6:30 with only a two-hour break at São Paulo coach station. The weather in Curitiba is perishing cold! John now has the flu, but should be alright in a couple of days.

The Wild West

Our most traumatic journey in Rondônia was to the remote township of Colorado, for the organisation of the local Baptist church. We did this long journey during our eight-month period of orientation in Porto Velho. It was the rainy season. As with all the roads, in every town outside the capital, there was no asphalt in Colorado; the shop fronts were just as they might have been in North America in the 1800s, with a rail to tether the horses in front of each of the numerous drinking saloons. Not exactly the place to be unwell, except that is exactly what happened. Maria had been given a cold orange drink, mixed with water. We always drank black coffee, *cafezinho,* when travelling, because we knew the water had been boiled, if not filtered. But so as not to offend, Maria accepted the drink. We had been given food all day and, in the evening, were served a big meal. One could not fault the hospitality of the local people. During that night Maria became unwell and needed to use the bathroom. There was no inside loo, no running water, and no electricity in the house. So, she made her way to the back door, where she found a bucket of water, there for the purpose. Armed with this in one hand and a kerosene lamp in the other, she made her way to the outside loo. It was raining. By next morning, Maria needed to call in the doctor but instead received a home visit from the local pharmacist. It was a dark, rainy day when an elderly, but kindly man, dressed in a long raincoat, with his trousers tucked inside his huge wellington boots, entered the room. Our eyes widened as he produced the syringe and sterilised the needle in boiling water. He administered the injection through a needle as long as your arm. The treatment worked, and amazingly she was soon feeling well enough to travel on.

On our journey home, we encountered a stretch of road that had been transformed into a field by the constant rain. A local farmer had come to the rescue with his tractor. He was able to negotiate the difficult conditions and tow us through this quagmire. Like us, several other vehicles were in the queue waiting their turn. We got out of our car, Maria, myself and Pastor Jacinto, our Brazilian companion on this journey from Porto Velho. As I took a few steps outside, so my feet sank ankle deep into the mud. Then, as I lifted my feet out of the mud, my shoes parted company with my feet and disappeared. My feet were by then covered in thick mud. I retrieved my shoes and, as I did so, an adventurous lorry driver decided to attempt to drive through without the aid of the tractor. As we stood by, watching the wheels of the lorry turning and sliding in the mud, suddenly a huge amount of mud and water came in my direction. It drenched me from head to toe. I was not amused. In abject frustration, I threw my shoes as far as I could, only to have to wade further into the mud to retrieve them a second time. The rest of our journey was done with a towel around my waist, as my trousers were no longer fit to wear. If we were to add anything to that miserable weekend, it would only be to say that Colorado do Oeste was the ugliest place we had ever seen - Wild West in the extreme, and known locally as *o fim do mundo,* the end of the world!

Enjoying a break from driving with Pastor Jacinto

Spiritual retreat

Most evangelical churches in Brazil hold a spiritual retreat during Carnival. In February 1980, the Baptist churches from Porto Velho joined together at a *chácara,* (a privately owned small holding out of town, with basic facilities). We enjoyed a wonderful time together, exploring the forest and swimming in the river. Though the retreat was mainly for the young people of the church, the older ones (still young at heart) joined in.

The men and boys slept outside under the stars, except for a temporary canvas cover to keep off the dampness of the night. The cool night air made it easier to sleep than if we had been indoors. I smothered myself in insect repellent, as I had been

43

warned that the little creatures with wings were to be feared more than the big cats that roamed deep in the forest. Our hammocks were slung from the trees around a clearing at the edge of the forest. One morning, some of the boys tried a prank by turning the occupants out of their hammocks. It was a rude awakening, both for me and one particular offender as I don't think that he knew that I was the occupant of the hammock he had selected to turn upside down!

Just before this, at Christmas 1979 we penned the following lines:

> We are enjoying our work among the churches in Porto Velho and in particular, the special responsibilities we have for the Liberdade Church, a small but lively group. We have also been impressed by the vitality of the young people from our Baptist churches here, who seem to have the happy knack of enjoying life to the full and always seeking ways to make Christ known through worship, fellowship and recreation. There is something very genuine about their faith; it is natural and spontaneous, and we give God thanks for them.

Long journey to hospital

Immediately after the retreat, Maria and I travelled to São Paulo for our annual Mission retreat. Then on to Paraná state for a short holiday. One day, as I was driving back through the mountains from the coast to

Curitiba, I felt unusually tired. The next day, we started out on our return journey to Porto Velho. The greatest part of this long journey from southeast to northwest Brazil was done by road. We changed buses in São Paulo and travelled overnight to Campo Grande in the west. We arrived there at seven in the morning, where we had breakfast at the local bus station. Then we were on the road again. It was on this leg of the journey that I became severely unwell. We arrived in Cuiabá late afternoon and were met by our colleagues David and Doris Doonan. Maria informed them of the situation, and they took us to their home. I had eaten nothing since breakfast and ate nothing that evening. In the morning it was decided that, as a precaution, I should see the doctor before catching the plane to Porto Velho. We entered the hospital waiting room, and soon I needed to lie down. Even sitting was impossible. As a result, the doctor called us in straight away. He did a clinical examination and said my liver was enlarged, and that I had hepatitis with possible malaria.

The next eight days were spent in a hospital bed. Blood tests eliminated the added complication of malaria. In Brazil, hepatitis is treated more proactively than in the United Kingdom. So I was on an intravenous drip, which was taken out each night and inserted again the next morning. By the last day in hospital they had run out of veins in my arms and hands. While in hospital, I was given a book to read by Doris Doonan about a young American couple, friends of C.S. Lewis. They were students at Oxford, and she became unwell and increasingly tired. Sadly, she did not get better and died of liver failure. It is remarkable how I was able to read through the whole book with the utmost peace of mind. One day a Brazilian pastor came to visit me. He wasted no time in telling me that if I had contracted hepatitis with malaria, I would most likely have died. The day before I was allowed out of hospital, on the Sunday, as the late afternoon sun was streaming burning hot through the window of my private ward (which it did every afternoon at that time), a Roman Catholic priest kindly came to visit and pray for me. As he was praying, he stepped backwards towards the fan which was giving some relief from the heat. Despite the pain, I was feeling in my arms and hands, and the heat of the room, the sound of cloth and blades whirling together made me laugh, almost too audibly, to both his embarrassment and mine.

Home again

After convalescing at the Doonan's home in Cuiabá for a further week, we set out on the last leg of our journey to Porto Velho. I had lost considerable weight and then suffered a temporary setback soon after we arrived home. We had been invited to a birthday party, but the excitement and frolics had proved too much for me. For the next few days, I was back in bed. A visit to the doctor and more blood tests followed. When we went back to get the blood test results, the doctor pronounced that I had the early stages of hepatitis. I was able to inform him that these symptoms were more likely the latter stages, and explained that I had already been treated for this in hospital. Why I didn't tell the doctor about this before I don't know. I think I assumed I had been cured of hepatitis and couldn't get it again.

An essential aspect of our ministry in Porto Velho was to visit some of the people around the town connected with the church, but for one reason or another not able to attend. For example, there was a lady called Raimunda.

This is what we wrote after a visit to her home:

She is a Christian and the mother of one of our church members, Precópio. She is completely housebound, being paralysed from the waist down. But she is very cheerful and manages to get around the house sliding in a sitting position. She cleans the house herself and has a small stool to sit on when cooking. When we were there at Christmastime, she had us singing all the carols in the hymn book, which was quite a lot of singing for four people! Another person we visited is a Catholic friend of a newly converted Christian. She is also paralysed from the waist down. However, the atmosphere in that house was completely different. Whereas Raimunda has accepted her disability and to some extent overcome it, this woman does not seem to be making any attempt to improve her situation. Is there not something for us to learn from this? When Jesus lives in the heart of a person, there is the strength and courage to grasp every day as a gift from him.

On another occasion, I preached at a congregation on the banks of the River Madeira, in Porto Velho. From the pulpit, as I looked through the main entrance to the building, I was almost distracted by the beauty of the view outside, as the fast-moving river glided through the emerald forest around. After the service, I remarked to the leader of the small riverside congregation that the setting was just as I had imagined a missionary setting would be. By the end of May, I felt well enough to drive the 440 miles to our first permanent missionary posting in Vilhena, on the border with the state of Mato Grosso.

Chapter Three

A sad tale

We were ready to set out from Porto Velho, on Tuesday morning, having spent the previous night in a hotel. The removal van had taken our furniture, appliances and boxes, so the house we had lived in, close to the airport, was now empty. That is except for our little puppy dog, who we named Waterloo. As we couldn't take him with us to the hotel, we left him with bedding, food and water, and on a good length of lead. We intended to collect him first thing in the morning. But when we arrived at the house next morning, he had gone. What is more, to our astonishment, not only was our dog missing, but also his bedding, food and lead. We searched the streets around our house, calling his name and looking in every garden. In the end, we had to give up, as we were losing precious time. From that moment, the long journey ahead was considerably longer. We naturally, kept wondering what had happened to our little friend. We were hoping that someone mistakenly thought he had been abandoned and had given him a new home.

Our biggest challenge yet

The journey through Rondônia took us two days. We stopped overnight halfway at a very basic hotel, though it was comfortable and clean. Thankfully, it was not like the one in Ouro Preto, where we stayed a year later, on our way to Porto Velho. There our sleep was disturbed by rats scampering around

Erosion plays havoc with
the roads in Rondônia

during the night. Needless to say, we didn't get much sleep. It was now the beginning of the dry season, south of the equator, so the road was passable but very dusty and full of potholes which had been caused by the rains of the previous six months.

A basic timber and iron bridge in Rondônia

On the second day of our journey, we drove straight into a giant pothole on the brow of a hill, and this was followed by another hidden crater. As the car virtually flew in the air into the crater, I was flung forward, banging my head on the metal frame supporting the windscreen. I still bear the scar on my forehead to this day. I remember Maria just laughed. How good it is that God gives us courage and a sense of humour in those situations. The car might well have been broken, and we would have been stranded without communication miles from anywhere, but miraculously it survived, and so did we.

We arrived at Vilhena in the late afternoon. I remember that it was the day of the European Football Cup Final, on 28th May 1980. Our emotions were of excitement and anticipation. Vilhena is a remote and distant place, hundreds of miles from the state capital.

Main Street, Vilhena 1980

The following is from a letter written at the time and describes our impressions on arriving there that day:

Vilhena has grown since our first visit twelve months ago and has become a more pleasant place in which to live. It is taking form and shape with new shops, a new hotel, somewhere to 'eat out', two new praças (town squares), new and attractive houses, facilities for recreational activities and a better and safer water supply; all this and the promise of 20km of asphalt within the town in the near future. For the moment, however, the dust is just as bad as ever, and as we live on the main road, we get our fair share of it in the house. Nothing stays clean for long. When we first came to Brazil, the dirt roads took some getting used to, but now we think nothing of it. Most things by way of essentials are obtainable in the town, although as in Porto Velho the shops offer a very limited choice and prices are higher than in other parts of the country. The climate is excellent with warm, sunny days and cool evenings. Medical facilities are poor in comparison with the large cities as was underlined recently when a young man died in hospital following a road accident. If doctors had had access to more sophisticated equipment such as exists in São Paulo, Rio de Janeiro and Curitiba, he might have lived.

The electricity supply to the town was only from six in the morning until midnight. Water shortages due to the primary pump breaking and new parts having to be ordered from São Paulo meant that we could be without tap water for two weeks at a time. Washing clothes in the river and taking drinking water from the local spring were the only way to keep clean and hydrated. But we mucked in with our neighbours and everybody else until all this became second nature and even good fun. Maria would fetch water from the spring together with Aparecida, an eleven-year-old girl, who lived in the house across the road from us. She and her two younger siblings, Leonice and Fátima, became like daughters to us. They would always be in our house. By the time Maria and Aparecida had got to the top of the hill, Maria had spilt half the contents of her bucket. Aparecida managed to get to the top with a full bucket, having perfected the art of water carrying through regular practice over a number of years.

In search of a better life

Our young friends,
Aparecida, Fátima and Leonice

A big surprise to us was the living conditions of our neighbours. We had rented a wooden house; almost all the houses in the town were of wood, as timber was a commodity in abundance. The inside walls were painted, and we enjoyed the modern convenience of a simple gas stove. Some of our church friends used wood fires inside their houses, the smoke blackening the ceiling. They relaxed on hard wooden benches, with just flimsy curtains, for privacy, into the adjoining bedrooms.

What we noticed most was that they were content and happy. Their seemingly deprived state contrasted to our comfortable western homes, and we were shocked that these apparent deprivations were of little importance to them. They were, in many ways, far richer than us, because they found real worth in family and friends, rather than things or material possessions. They told us that they had come here in search of a better life. It makes one wonder what they had left behind.

The Baptist congregation

Baptist Congregation, Vilhena

The Baptist congregation, like the town itself, was quite small. It was, however, in a strategic location on the main highway through northwest Brazil. This is how we described the situation on our arrival:

The congregation for which we are responsible has just fifteen members. It is situated at one end of the town and consists of a simple wooden building with gas lighting. We have, in fact, been wired up for electricity, but await permission to be connected to the town's generator. Baptist work was started in Vilhena about four years ago by a Brazilian missionary sent from a church in São Paulo. Owing to the more rapid growth of a neighbouring church for which he was also responsible, he was able to give only a small amount of time to the cause here. Hence, it remained weak while the other grew stronger. Nevertheless, we have quickly come to realise that given encouragement, folk here will rise to the challenge ahead. In July we are to have an outreach campaign lasting for about twelve days, during which time Pastor Lino from the São Paulo church will be with us. Plans are also in hand for a new church building appropriate to the task God has given us. We are fortunate in having a full-time evangelist working with us. His name is Ranofo, he is twenty-one years of age and hopes to train for the ministry after completing his basic education next year. He is a source of encouragement to us, and we thank God for him.

The new wooden building was finished by the time we left for a short break in England the following September. I must have unloaded, lifted and handled every item of material that went into the new construction. More importantly, new people were coming into the church from south and mid-west Brazil, and also São Paulo. We remember when we first arrived there that the men sat on one side of the church and the women on the other. Even married couples were separated in this way. We didn't see any point in changing this and did it really matter. But as new families began to arrive, the married couples among them did sit together, and eventually, the younger original members of the congregation followed suit. There is a saying: 'Change what you can, accept what you can't, and be wise to know the difference.' As in this particular case, some things will change anyway, in their own time.

We parked in their bedroom
A year later, we were moving house. The owner of our house had decided to double the rent, though our Mission would willingly have paid the increase, we began looking for alternative accommodation. We found a brand new wooden house, two, in fact, side by side a few streets away. These properties overlooked a forest, which was the other side of a small stream.

We decided to do our own removal. The removal process would require several short journeys to our new house. We borrowed a small truck from a family who attended the Baptist church. The truck was perfect for the task at hand; however, it had no foot brake. We managed to transfer our items of furniture and domestic appliances from our old house to our new one, even though this meant negotiating a gentle downward hill to get there. Everything went like clockwork, until our final journey when we were taking the truck back to its owners. They lived in a small wooden house on a corner plot on a road with a marked downward slope. As we approached their house, I applied the handbrake. This method of stopping had served us excellently all afternoon and evening. The truck was now unloaded, but as we sought to bring it to a halt alongside the house, it continued on its downward trajectory into the side of the house, where the family were, by now, fast asleep. With a loud bang and crunch, it came to a halt slightly entering the main bedroom. We were horrified, and naturally, they were alarmed by our sudden intrusion into their peaceful night. They really should have been annoyed about our careless driving, but not a word of reproach was spoken by any of the family. Our words of apology were so graciously accepted. In fact, we were more annoyed with ourselves, than ever they were with us.

The seed is planted

The small congregation that we had inherited in May 1980 met in a tiny wooden structure measuring eight metres by five metres. The congregation began to grow, and we decided to build another structure in front of the first. At the church meeting where the decision was taken to build, one of the members expressed concern as to how we would raise the money to pay for the new structure. He pointed out, quite rightly, that we were still relatively few in numbers. I suggested that a better approach might be to consider the opportunities before us, rather than the problems. The vote that we should go ahead was almost unanimous, except for this one solitary figure.

A year later, one evening, this same gentleman and I arrived at church together. We were the first to arrive. He was the one who opened the doors of the building before each service. As he did so on this particular evening, he looked at me and said: 'Pastor we need to build again.' This was an incredible moment, among many others, during our thirty-three years of service in Brazil. Here was a man, a devout follower of the Lord Jesus, who had seen for himself that when God places a challenge before us, he also provides the means. We do not necessarily have to have the means at the start. The whole exciting thing about faith is that we follow him, trusting him for the outcome.

Christmas dinner

It was our second Christmas in Vilhena, and we had been invited to have Christmas dinner with one of our church families. As we sat at the dinner table, a long wooden structure for a large family gathering, the centrepiece was a decorated hog's head with an apple stuffed in its mouth. To have this creature looking at us while we ate the rest of him was a little surreal. But he tasted really good, and we had no trouble finishing the meal. That December afternoon, we drove back to our own house, in the summer sunshine, well satisfied with the experience of sharing that special day with a family, many thousands of miles from our own families in England.

We prefer oven ready

Talking of meals, one day I was visiting a couple who gave me a live cockerel to take home. They meant us to eat it but to do that we would have had to kill it first. This was a step too far for us raised in the city. We, in fact, turned a corner of our back garden into a chicken run, found the cockerel a hen and raised the family they produced. I even learnt how to clip their wings, to stop the young chickens flying over the fence into our neighbours' gardens. Every so often, we would give one of the chickens to our neighbour, who returned it to us on a plate, ready to go into the oven.

A good start

At Christmas 1980, we wrote home. No doubt with longings to be with our family in England at that time of year and dreaming of a 'White Christmas.' Here we reflected on how it was for us so many miles away:

We have six candidates preparing for baptism and shall be holding an open-air baptismal service before Christmas. We have now completed the building of our church extension, and this has generated great enthusiasm among the people. It was a magnificent effort on their part and a step of faith truly blessed of God. In three months £1,000 has been raised with the help of a £300 loan from the Colorado church nearby. Apart from the loan repayment, all accounts have been settled – not bad for a congregation of fifteen who, a year ago, were in desperate need of some inspiration. Unfortunately, our evangelist, Ranofo, is soon leaving us. One of the churches in Porto Velho has invited him to be responsible for its young people's work. We shall miss him a good deal, but are grateful for the time he spent with us.

We are happy to report that Vilhena continues to grow and prosper. Each week new families arrive with the hope of beginning a new life in this rapidly developing area. Since we arrived at the end of May, six new Baptist families have moved into the town and are now worshipping with us and contributing to the life of the church. With new folk coming into membership by profession of faith or by transfer, we anticipate an increase of 100% by the turn of the year. Two house groups have commenced in the town, one of which located on the industrial estate where there is no other Christian witness either Catholic or Protestant. The young people have organised themselves under the leadership of Sr. Esmeraldinho, who is bringing experience and imagination to the task. The women's work is going well, and the ladies enjoy meeting in one another's homes, especially if there is something special to celebrate like a new arrival This also gives them the opportunity to invite along their neighbours and non-committed friends to hear the Gospel and to pray together.

Once the rains started in mid-August, it became extremely difficult to leave town by road. The roads wouldn't improve until the next dry season, beginning in mid-May the following year, and each year they got worse.

To give you an example, when we first arrived in Vilhena we could do the two-hundred-and-eight-mile journey to Ji-Paraná (about half-way to Porto Velho)

Washing the car - Vilhena

in a day. A year later, we could only get as far as Pimenta Bueno on the first day, a journey of 118 miles. By our second year in Rondônia, the seasonal rains had all but washed away the road between Vilhena and Pimenta Bueno. A diversion had to be created to avoid Vilhena being cut off entirely from the north. It was just before Easter when we wrote our next letter home:

We are now coming to the end of the rainy season, which, as usual, brought virtually all movement of traffic on the notorious BR 364 highway to a standstill. This road has no asphalt and is at best a dirt track embedded with rock boulders and at worst no road at all where the mud and sand have been washed away by the continuous intense tropical rain.

This has meant for us a time of more concentrated effort in Vilhena, building up and encouraging the little group of believers we found on our first visit here in 1979.

At our members' meeting in February, we received ten applications for membership. This has encouraged us, and our membership now stands at 31 with two further applications anticipated and three candidates for baptism on Easter Sunday. We have discovered an idyllic spot deep in the forest where the river runs pure and clear and cold.

Once a month we meet at our preaching point on the industrial estate on the edge of town. (A preaching point is the first phase of a new church plant). The Christian lady in whose house we meet had a major operation a year ago which saved her life and she has seized on this as an opportunity to tell others about the goodness and love of God.

We are fortunate in having several school teachers in membership with us, and at the end of January, two of them, together with Maria, led our first Holiday Bible Club. Eighty children came with an average daily attendance of fifty. Many were children who already come to the church, but a few who didn't are now with us at Sunday school each week.

The local authorities are starting a new housing development in the next few months, and we have already made an application for a piece of land. In order to reinforce our application, I, together with another member of the church, met the mayor in his office at the Town Hall. We were introduced to him by a lawyer whose wife worships with us. During our meeting with the mayor, we were shown the plans for the future development of the town and enjoyed the traditional 'cafezinho' (black coffee), a mark of Brazilian hospitality. We then read from the Bible and prayed together.

We were privileged to count as our friends several key people in the town, including a medical doctor who worked at the local Santa Helena hospital, and the owner of two of the town's hotels. These friendships were significant for us personally. As in most communities, it is good to know those who are central to the life of the population, and also to be known by them, especially in a small town like Vilhena. Fifteen years later, Melkisedek, whose story we share in the next chapter, became mayor of Vilhena. He then served as mayor for a second term, from 2001-2004. By that time Vilhena had grown almost beyond recognition. It was good to have been there in those early pioneer days and to contribute to its future through the local church.

Chapter Four

A packed house

A year later, on Good Friday 1982, an American missionary in the town had a Billy Graham film about the land of Israel. The small church building was packed to overflowing. People who usually did not go to church came to see the show. In 1982 this was still a novelty in the interior of Brazil. People were gathered outside the door and around the building looking through the windows. The film on a large spool arrived and the evening's proceedings began. Maria had gone to fetch some folk in our small jeep, so had to make several journeys backwards and forwards. By the time she arrived with the last group, the show had started. She stood at the door of the church looking in. To her surprise, Cliff Richard starred in the film, and so she started to push her way forward into the building in order to get a better view. As she was the pastor's wife, everyone made way for her. When she arrived at the front of the church, she was immediately offered a seat where someone else was already sitting; this was the one and only time that she used her status as the pastor's wife to her advantage.

The President comes to town

One day, the whole town was full of even greater excitement. The last of the military presidents of Brazil, General João Baptista de Oliveira Figueiredo, was coming to open the new airport. The old airport, which we had used on more than one occasion, to get to Porto Velho or Cuiabá, had a short dirt airstrip running alongside the main street, and could cope only with the Bandeirantes planes, as they are known in Brazil. These had a seating capacity of nineteen passengers. Apart from this model of plane, only smaller ones, such as the single-engined Cessna could land and take off. The new airport was built to accommodate larger planes, like the Boeing 737, to come and go. At the old and new airports, the passengers, as well as the baggage, had to be weighed. We noticed that the heavier passengers were not charged any excess.

After the inaugural speech given by the President, we were all treated to a *churrasco* (barbeque) paid for by the President, or by the government, whichever you prefer. The official party then went off to the newest and best hotel in town for lunch. I recall how the President would address the crowd as *'meus patrícios'*, or 'my fellow countrymen.' Every Brazilian President has a distinctive way of addressing their compatriots; this was his. A memorable day, for a small 'one-horse town', as Vilhena was once described by a visiting film producer from Old England.

A miraculous recovery
Some 78 miles from Vilhena is the municipality of Cerejeiras. Sr. Marcos lives there and owns a coffee farm. One day, he came to our house in Vilhena, with his daughter Raquel. They invited us to spend a few days with them in Cerejeiras. Sr. Marcos was a

leading light in the community and a Baptist from the local congregation. We gladly accepted their invitation to visit the farm and the other members of the family.

The following is what we wrote home shortly after our visit:

Upon our arrival just after dark, we found that a service was being held in his house and many Baptist and other folk had come. We had a small part in the service which was in thanksgiving for the recovery of one of Sr. Marcos' children (Melkisedek), who had contracted malaria and as a result of the treatment being given him, he nearly died. He was put in an oxygen tent in the local hospital and was given artificial respiration on the journey there by one of his sisters. He was upheld by the prayers of his family who wanted to share their story with friends and neighbours. After the service, we were invited by numerous folk to conduct services in their homes. In fact, four services were arranged for us. This kept us very busy, and on one occasion I walked eight kilometres while Maria rode on the back of a bicycle to the house where the service was to be held. On each occasion we were given hospitality before the rest of the folk arrived. This gave us the opportunity of getting to know something of the background of these people and the conditions in which they lived.

No electricity, just small oil lamps; no running water, but from the well or river; no gas for cooking, but an open wood fire; no bathroom or toilet in some cases, just a secluded place in the undergrowth.

Sr. Marcos and his family treated us like royalty, and most of the time while on their farm we drank coffee,

Cerejeiras forest stream

ate pawpaw and sampled, in excess, the pineapple which also grew in abundance. This extravagance had the inevitable effect of confining us both to the

Logging in the Amazon Rainforest

outside loo for most of the night. One of the highlights of any trip into the forest is to find a clear, cold stream for a refreshing dip during the heat of the day. This was no exception on our visit to Cerejeiras. Sr. Marcos' family were wonderful hosts and gave us the experience of our lives.

Exotic sights

Our many years in Brazil brought us into contact with the exotic fruits and crops that are available to buy in our UK supermarkets; however, most people have never seen them growing in their natural habitat. Not only on Sr. Marcos' farm but also walking through the cool forest, we saw pineapple growing along a pathway leading to the small thatched mud house of a Brazilian Christian family in Chupinguaia. In the surrounding forest, straining our necks, we looked upwards into the sky and were amazed at the height and rectitude of the Brazil nut tree (*castanha do Pará*). In the south of Brazil, we were surrounded by citrus fruit bearing trees, with oranges, tangerines and lemons growing in our own garden in Rio Negro.

Growing coffee in the rainforest

On the coastal plain of Paraná there were bananas growing in abundance, wild jasmine forming hedgerows of white and green, flame red poinsettias in full bloom by the roadside in mid-winter, and multi-coloured busy lizzies thriving beneath the rock face of the *Serra do Mar*. Tobacco was cultivated on the high plateau in the fields around our church in Roseira. Then in the northeast, the unforgettable sight of sugar cane plantations along the road to Natal. These are among the sights and experiences that have forever impressed their images upon our minds. Brazil may be a land of contrasts and contradictions, but it is clothed in regal beauty. From the tree covered mountains and sweetly scented pine forests of the south to the sparkling, azure sea of the northeast, to the canopy of the emerald rainforest, in the far north.

Axle deep in mud

Another incredible experience was on one of our trips to Chupinguaia, a community deep in the Brazilian rainforest. This time we travelled in our mini jeep. The poor condition of the roads meant an eleven-hour journey to this isolated outpost of Baptist life in Brazil. Although we had a jerry can attached to the back of our vehicle containing an extra five gallons of petrol, this was only enough for emergencies. It was not sufficient to get us there and back, and there were no petrol stations once we left Vilhena.

The only way we could do that journey independently was to accept the offer of petrol from our hosts, who had brought in supplies from Pimenta Bueno, their nearest town. Our vehicle, with its canvas roof and plastic windows, was also equipped with a spade as standard for digging ourselves out of the deep, engulfing sand along the remote forest tracks. As we approached the village, it was getting dark. We were almost there when in front of us the road became a lake. We stopped to assess the situation and poking into the muddy water with a stick, we agreed the best way through the expanse of water before us. The passengers, Maria and a young woman from Vilhena, whose family lived in the village we were heading for, went through on foot, as I drove into the water. The engine laboured as I put my foot down on the accelerator, slowed, skidded and shuddered, before coming to a halt in deep sand and mud. The more I accelerated, the further the wheels sank into the ground beneath, until they were

CHUPINGUAIA

almost entirely submerged.

The remainder of our journey was completed on foot, with our Brazilian companion reassuring us at regular intervals that we were nearly there until we eventually emerged from the pitch dark forest into the village and safety. That same night, I returned to the scene of our misfortune with a group of local men to retrieve our vehicle. With their help, it was soon pulled out of the muddy mire using a strong rope and a four by four, which, incidentally, ours wasn't.

Going the extra mile

On the Sunday, we conducted worship in the small church building made of wood with a mud lining around the walls to keep it cool, and a roof made from dried palms. I spent much of the day retrieving the car (which had been left overnight near the few houses and a small shop in the centre of the forest settlement) and having it repaired. But this was little hardship compared to one woman who walked over a mile to church that morning and back home again to prepare lunch. She repeated the journey in the afternoon for the ladies meeting and in the evening, was back at church again with her children – one in arms.

Get me to the church on time

On another visit to Chupinguaia, where I was attending a wedding, our transport was a lorry, which we were assured always broke down on this journey. The outward journey was surprisingly uneventful, as the truck and its driver negotiated with consummate ease the narrow, winding, sandy track through the cool forest. From the main dirt road, it was a further twenty-eight miles to this isolated village, a total journey of ninety miles. It took the best part of a day to get there. If our journey that day was uneventful, our weekend in Chupinguaia was definitely not.

Next day was one of the most extraordinary we can remember. In the morning preparations for the wedding-breakfast were in full swing. The women prepared the food which was set on long tables under a marquee. While they were doing this, the men went off to make provision for the meat course. Into the piggery, we went, where several unfortunate animals were selected to be slaughtered. A single knife thrust into the pig's heart and the job was done. Well, if only it were. The squealing pigs seemed to take ages to succumb, though by the third or fourth the sight became almost commonplace. Even so, it was something that I will never forget.

In the afternoon, we witnessed a baptism in the local river. One of the candidates was the bridegroom to be married to his bride that evening. It was a joyous event as we stood on the river bank watching, as one by one the candidates made their profession of faith and were immersed in the river.

Baptisms in the river in Chupinguaia

The hour for the wedding ceremony soon came round. Everything was ready. There was a problem, though. The registrar had not arrived. His presence was vital for the wedding to have legal credence.

The elders of the church met with the visiting minister to decide what to do. One possibility was to call the wedding off. The non-appearance of the registrar was a most embarrassing and awkward moment. Finally, the decision was taken to go ahead with the wedding and for the couple to travel to the registry office after the festivities, to be legally married the following morning. To make sure that the newlyweds did not commit any sin on their wedding night, but before they were legally married, the presiding minister travelled with them and stayed with them until the following morning.

Our longest walk

We remained in the village until after the weekend, enjoying the generous hospitality of our hosts. It had been an eventful weekend, but there was another surprise awaiting us. We boarded the same lorry, the one that always broke down, but didn't on our outward journey, and began the long journey back home. This time we got on the back of the lorry like everyone else, sitting on huge sacks of rice, which were to be sold in town. On the outward journey, we were the only passengers and so enjoyed the luxury of sitting in the cab with the driver. As we bumped and swayed over the uneven terrain and made our way through the forest towards the main road, the lorry came to a halt; the engine had cut out and would not start up again. It soon became apparent that the only way out was on foot. This was no problem to begin with; however, as the morning turned into afternoon, and then early evening, we sensed we had a situation on our hands. We realised we had been walking slower than the rest (because we had a heavy case to carry with all the things we missionaries needed for a long weekend – never again!) and had lost sight of those in front of us.

Without water, we stopped by a forest stream to rest, and in order to quench our thirst, we cupped our hands and stooped to drink from the stream. The water was crystal clear, and against all medical advice from BMS headquarters in London, we drank several times before taking off our shoes and socks and getting in the water to cool down. As it began to grow dark, thoughts of spending the night under the stars had already entered our minds. At that precise moment, there was the sound of a truck approaching from the right just ahead of us. I ran the short distance, ahead of Maria, towards the junction in the forest. We still had about eight miles to walk before we reached the main road. We explained to the driver how our lorry had broken down and gratefully accepted a lift. How much of a coincidence was that? Although it was only a truck and its driver, it was also what we call a God-incidence. What were the chances of us being there at that very moment after hours trekking through the forest? Had we not been in the presence of God the whole time? At that exact moment was he not walking alongside us, as much and as real as when Jesus joined the two disciples on the Emmaus Road, on the first Easter Sunday evening? Soon after, we caught up with the rest of our company. There wasn't room on the back of the truck for everybody, but we did persuade the driver to stop and pick up a pregnant woman and her husband. They, like the rest of us, had been walking through the forest for most of the day. This particular couple were moving house to live in the town and had with them less luggage than we had taken for the weekend. So, as it happened, we were the first to arrive at the point where another lorry was to take us the rest of the journey home. An important lesson was learned that day: take with you on your journey as little baggage as possible, especially if you go into the jungle. But more important still, even when we are ill-prepared for what lies ahead, God is always one step ahead of every circumstance. That day, like on so many others, we found God in Brazil.

A miracle in the rainforest

We have lasting memories of our visits to Chupinguaia. On one of these visits, we were asked to go to the home of a family who lived in a small clearing. The wooden house was as simple as you could imagine, and the family enjoyed only the very basics of modern day living. The reason for the visit was that a small child had been unwell for several days and had not eaten. By now the child was weak and the family desperate. There were no medical facilities within miles. I was asked if I would pray over the child. As the child lay in a hammock, which was strung between two trees in the cool of the front garden, I prayed God's healing for the child. We concluded our visit and that same day returned home. Some days later, we received word from the village that immediately we had left, the child had eaten some food and was getting stronger every day. God had heard our prayer and reached out to this child. Not that this is always the outcome, as you will see from other stories in this book. But this is one token that he is there, and he is not silent, to quote the title of a Francis Schaeffer book. For the rest, we have to trust him. But God gives us enough to go on doing exactly that.

Fire, fire!

One weekend, when we visited the congregation in Chupinguaia, we stayed, as usual, in the home of one of the leaders of that small community. He and his family went out for an hour or so, and we stayed behind. As it became dark, we decided to ignite the one source of light in the room; a paraffin lamp with a wick. We refilled it as it had run dry and lit a match. But, the flame caught the vapour of the paraffin and suddenly the one piece of luxury in the house, a linen tablecloth, was alight. We managed to put out the flames, but how would we explain this to our hosts on their return home? Their gracious and forgiving acceptance of the incident remains with us to this day. The reaction of the family was so characteristic of the humble poor in Brazil, in whose lives we could see the outworking of the grace and forgiveness of God.

A swarm of locusts

The rains began in August and were at their most intense during the months of January and February. Between May and August, it didn't rain at all. It was then that we could do most of our travelling out of town by road, giving us a sense of freedom once again. But the dry season also brought with it something else. We would occasionally take a drive for a few miles into the country to visit an indigenous, though virtually westernised tribe (before they were forced to move on by another tribe), or perhaps to visit the nearby indigenous museum or escape to some local beauty spot. On these outings, we would often notice what looked like a dark blanket spread out across the road in front of us. As we got closer, we could see that this apparent blanket was, in fact, alive with locusts; thousands of them. There was no alternative route, so I had to drive straight at them. As we did so, they flew into the air in front of us and all around us. Our mini jeep had a canvas roof with nothing more than flimsy plastic flaps as windows. The swarm of locusts was so dense that inevitably many of these hideous creatures got inside our vehicle and started flying about around our heads. Once through the worst of it, we would spend the next five minutes or so trying to get rid of them out of the windows. After a while, we got used to this, and it became great fun doing battle with the locusts. One afternoon, however, I was looking out of our living room window. It was wide open as usual on those hot, dry afternoons. As I looked across the roofs of the neighbouring houses, I could see a huge black cloud moving from south to north across the blue sky. At first, I wasn't sure what it was. As I focussed my attention on what I was looking at, I realised that this unusual cloud was a gigantic swarm of locusts. I had never seen anything like it before, and have not seen anything like it since. It was a disturbing, heart-racing sight. If they had come our way, they would have covered every inch of ground around us, including the entire outside of the house, for sure. It was reminiscent of the scene from Alfred Hitchcock's film, 'The Birds', except there were millions of these locusts. They flew in a precise and tightly knit formation, across the sky, before my unbelieving eyes. They were doubtless on their way to wreak havoc and destruction in some poor unsuspecting farmer's fields. I wasted no further time in closing all the windows in our house – just in case.

Some important decisions

Amid all this excitement, we saw our small church grow from fifteen members to fifty within two years,

Clearing the road in the rainforest, near Vilhena

and it was now in a financial position to invite a Brazilian pastor. It was organised as a church on 3rd July 1982 and received the name of Centenary Baptist Church. The name chosen was to commemorate the centenary year of the founding of the first Baptist church in Brazil, in the city of Salvador. A special service was arranged, and the church members had to respond to questions about the nature of a church and Christian doctrine. Having satisfactorily answered the questions, they were accepted as a church in full-standing. There was some discussion as to what the name of the church should be. Although the majority accepted the unique opportunity of being called the Centenary Baptist

Church, a few still wanted the traditional name of First Baptist Church, as it was the first to be organised in our town by Baptists of the Brazilian Baptist Convention. However, the decision had already been taken at a church meeting, and that decision carried the day. Apparently, the debate didn't end there, and a year later there were further attempts to adopt the name of First Baptist Church. This was in case another church came along and called itself by that name. So a visit was made to the church by the Executive Director of the state Baptist Convention, who explained that they were the First Baptist Church but legally registered as the Centenary Baptist Church. It was explained that legally no future church could take the name of First Baptist Church.

The Vilhena congregation was not always an easy place to be during our time there. We lost out on acquiring a free piece of land from the local council because the men were unhappy that we had applied for this land in the name of the Baptist congregation and not the mother church in São Paulo. They felt that the land could not legally belong to the congregation, if the congregation was still not a legal entity registered with the Brazilian government. They even thought that I might have requested the land in my own name. The Municipal Secretary for Public Works assured us that, so far as they were concerned, the land had been requested in the name of the local Baptist congregation, with me as its representative. Still, the men voted not to proceed with the acquisition of this land. The women of the congregation, on the other hand, voted unanimously to go ahead. With such a divided vote, we decided not to proceed.

The acquisition of the land would have undoubtedly meant some considerable expense required to fund the new building project. The town council would not have allowed us to simply sit on it so building work would have to commence fairly well immediately. As it so happened, in future years, the town developed in a different direction, and a new church was required in another area of Vilhena, where a significant housing development had taken place. The particular side of town where we had hoped to invest remains virtually the same today as it was then, and nothing has really happened. So, disappointing though it was at the time, the right decision was taken.

Our furthest journey west
Anticipating our return to Brazil after a home assignment, we had been invited by the Rondônia-Acre Baptist Convention to work with the Second Baptist Church in Guajará-Mirim on the River Mamoré. The river divides Brazil from Bolivia and passes through one of the most remote areas of Brazil. Guajará-Mirim is an old colonial town with mainly brick built houses and shops. Despite its remoteness, Guajará-Mirim had asphalt roads and proper pavements, quite unlike any other town outside the capital, Porto Velho. By contrast, on the

opposite side of the river, the Bolivian town of Guayaramerin was dusty and basic. It did have countless, efficient motorbike taxis, which we both had the opportunity of using. We were taken by a delightful Bolivian missionary to the home of a member of the local Baptist congregation. It was there that we experienced our first (and last) glass of sweet corn juice, with its distinctly granular texture. It is definitely an acquired taste, though apparently a local favourite. Sweet corn was initially cultivated in southern Mexico and is widely eaten in central and South America. The idea was that we should serve the two churches on either side of the river. We observed that the road and rail link ended in Guajará-Mirim, beyond which there was only jungle. So no-one would be passing through, as it were. Neither was it a town that people were moving into in droves, as in Vilhena. In addition, there were already two Baptist churches on the Brazilian side of the river, and these had apparently fallen out with each other. We had our misgivings but accepted the invitation.

Guajará-Mirim was so different from Vilhena regarding its location and prospects for future growth. It did, though, hold an exceptional charm and was more established than Vilhena, at that point in time. As it happened, things didn't work out as planned. Our return from England was delayed due to the circumstances described in the Prologue. A Brazilian missionary pastor then came forward and offered to take up that particular challenge. For all our misgivings, we were disappointed not to be going to Guajará-Mirim, but could see the hand of God upon both that situation and our own future.

At the end of September 1982, we boarded a twin-engine plane belonging to the Amazon Basin Air Company (TABA), to begin our first home assignment in the United Kingdom. As our plane climbed into the afternoon sky over Vilhena, we had no inkling that we would not be returning to work in northwest Brazil.

Chapter Five

Our darkest day

Reginald Harvey, our General Director, greeted us on our return to London with the words, 'Mission accomplished.' A sense of achievement prevailed, and we were looking forward to sharing our first experiences of Brazil with the supporting churches around the United Kingdom.

Our first home assignment, however, was marked by personal tragedy. Our lovely daughter Joana-Maria was still-born on 1st October 1983. This was undoubtedly the hardest moment in our lives. I arrived at the Greenwich General Hospital to collect Maria, after what should have been a routine prenatal check-up. As I walked through the hospital entrance toward the unit where Maria had been attending, a nurse approached me. She informed me that there was something wrong with the baby and took me through to where Maria was waiting. It was then that the full truth emerged as Maria told me that we had lost the baby. It was impossible to take in the news that I had been given. 'But how?' I remember asking. There was no audible heartbeat, and this was confirmed by an ultrasound examination. We were allowed to go home to try and assimilate this profound life-changing tragedy. That night, as we were in bed, Maria asked me to pray. I said I didn't know how to pray in the situation facing us. When the words did come, I simply asked God to send us an angel as a token of his presence. The next morning, we went back to the hospital, where Maria was given medication to induce labour. She was also given an epidural so as not to endure the pain of childbirth. The hospital began the medication at eight o'clock in the morning. Maria gave birth to a beautiful, but lifeless baby girl the following day at six in the morning. The hospital staff wrapped the baby in a towel and gave her to me to hold. She had purple lips from asphyxia. Just one month before full-term the umbilical cord had wrapped itself round the baby's neck and deprived her of oxygen. As I took her, I said to Maria, 'She looks just like an angel.' Maria replied, 'Do you remember what you prayed for last night?' It was a spine-tingling moment. I knew then that God was in that situation more intimately than I could ever have imagined. The angel I had asked him to send to us was our baby daughter herself. She was the angel that God had sent us, but already taken to join the rest of his angels in heaven. I am quite convinced that she has been present in many other situations in our lives. If she had not been, I would not be here now to tell the story. We had already chosen her name, and later that day I was given a form to sign. But the form did not contain the baby's name. I refused to sign until her name had been added. The hospital duly complied, and I signed the form with tears and a broken heart. The worst thing I had to experience was waking up in the morning, and this went on for a number of days. It brought back all the pain, which sleep had taken away. At that time, still-born babies were generally dealt with by the hospital. We chose to bury our daughter ourselves.

Our good friend Edwin Boddington, my mentor during our first pastorate in Birmingham, conducted the simple service of internment at St Paul's New Churchyard, near Tunbridge Wells. Some other members of my family, on my mother's side, were buried there, and my mother was born in the nearby village of Rusthall. For some reason, we chose to go it alone. There were just Maria and myself at the burial, and Edwin and Mr Cook, the churchwarden, who closed the grave. Going through the formalities of burial was necessary for the healing process to begin in us. Shortly after, there was a programme on television called, *The Lost Babies*. It was about situations like our own. The parents who were featured in the programme did not know what had happened to their babies. They were unable to get over their grief until they did. Fortunately, they were able to discover where their babies had been buried. Then, and only then, did the healing process begin for those parents. We are comforted in that we did this for our baby.

Starting over

We eventually returned to Brazil on 10th June 1984. We happened to be on the same plane as the English football team's supporters. They were going to the game between England and Brazil in Rio de Janeiro. The match took place in the world-famous Maracanã Stadium, within the gaze of Christ the Redeemer, high up on the Corcovado Mountain. As it turned out, England won the game 2-0 in a historic victory to mark our return to Brazil.

We spent a couple of days in Rio and felt immediately at home in the balmy, laid-back atmosphere of that tropical city. We then caught the plane south to Curitiba on our way to Rio Negro, our next location. This was a far cry from the Amazon region, the scene of our earlier work in Brazil. This time we were situated on a plateau, in the southern state of Paraná. Rio Negro was located on the banks of the river of the same name. The river divides the states of Paraná and Santa Catarina. The population of Rio Negro is mostly of German descent, resulting from European migration patterns of the previous two centuries. We arrived in Rio Negro towards the end of June, in the depths of a Brazilian winter. Standing in front of our house in the early mornings, the view was obliterated by dense fog, which lifted only shortly before midday. The nights were cold, and a hard frost covered the ground at dawn. The very first morning, two ladies from the church arrived at our front door asking if there was anything they could do to help. My first thought was to answer: 'Could you change the weather?' How different this was from Rondônia where it was hardly ever cold. Even so, in Rio Negro, the month of January was hot, very hot, with long sunny days from morning to evening. It wasn't until the sun had gone down that the day cooled to any degree. Those were the 'lazy days' of a southern Brazilian summer.

Nature's healing power

We were responsible for two very different churches; one in Rio Negro, the other five miles out of town in the farming community of Roseira. The mother church, near the town centre, was sixty years old and Roseira, the daughter church, was ten years younger. The Executive Director of the Paraná Baptist Convention spoke at our welcome meeting in Roseira when we officially began our ministry there. He was clearly delighted that we had accepted the invitation to work there, and during his address to the gathered company exclaimed, 'God is Brazilian!' I understood him to mean that God has a very special place in his heart for Brazil. I believe that to be true. In Brazil, our eyes were opened to God's dealings with us and through us. We found him to be present and active when we least expected.

It was fascinating to observe the farming techniques in Roseira. These were from days gone by. The sight of a horse-drawn plough at work in the month of July, preparing the ground for the following year's crops of maize, beans and tobacco, drew me and my camera like a magnet. The tobacco crop would be sold to British American Tobacco, which has a factory in Rio Negro. This facility is a major provider of employment in the town. In mid-summer, at the beginning of the year, driving past fields of maize standing tall, as if reaching for the sky, proportioned one of my favourite vistas. Vast swathes of pine forests provided a dark and mysterious backcloth to the roadside pampas grasses, swaying in the summer breeze.

Horse-drawn plough - Roseira

Baptism at Roseira

These peaceful surroundings, as well as two loving and caring churches, were just what the doctor ordered for that moment in our lives. I once rode in a horse-drawn cart, driven by Sr. Zé, the oldest member of our Roseira church. Strange as it may seem, this was one of the most peaceful and calming experiences of my life. This very traditional setting turned out to be a special place and heralded a significant change of direction for our work in Brazil.

A new vision

The challenge of being responsible for two churches simultaneously provided an ideal opportunity to train local church leaders. Both the Rio Negro and Roseira churches had capable and dedicated leaders, but without any formal or even informal preparation. A young married man at the Roseira church had unmistakeable preaching gifts. He was a popular figure in the community and respected by the church. We saw the potential of this situation and encouraged João Pires to develop his God-given talents. He began a distance learning Bible course, and so his preparation to lead the church was underway.

João became the church evangelist and assisted at baptisms. These were held at a place where a small stream flowed into a deeper and wider area surrounded by a grassy embankment. The tank (*tanque*), as it was known, was an ideal location for baptisms by immersion in accordance with the New Testament tradition. On one occasion, as the candidates entered and left the water, our evangelist's discomfort became conspicuous. Afterwards, he explained that a fish had been nibbling away at his bare toes; an idea for bait when out fishing, maybe?

Putting the cart before the horse

Though we conducted several baptismal services in this community, there were no weddings; not that there was a lack of courting couples. The idea of simply moving in was fairly common practice among people outside of the church, though not so among church-goers. The wedding of a girl in our church to a lad who was not from the church had been agreed with the church and the date set. Unfortunately, the couple, like many others, could not wait for the day to arrive and anticipated the honeymoon, which, in rural Brazil, ruled out a church wedding.

Though disappointing, these were relatively secondary issues. We could not change popular culture overnight and did not see it as our purpose to do so. There were, however, cultural issues within the church which we felt we should start to deal with, if only by chipping away at the surface. In this respect, we were mostly successful. The notion that all the people of God had received a God-given vocation was central to our vision, though this was not generally understood by Brazilian Baptists at the time. Our work towards this understanding of the people of God began in Roseira; it became the guiding principle for our future ministry in Brazil.

Nothing new under the sun

Our colleagues Roy and Margaret Connor had served these two churches immediately before us. During their ministry, a new church building had been completed in Rio Negro, to replace the old wooden structure that had existed there since the church was founded. Roy and Margaret captivated people in the church and community. Roy was a charismatic preacher and Margaret, a caring pastor's wife. The year before we arrived, there had been severe flooding. The river had burst its banks and inundated large swathes of the town. Roy had worked tirelessly to bring relief to those who had suffered the loss of possessions at that time. He was the link person between the local community in Rio Negro and the wider Brazilian Baptist family who sent food, clothing and blankets to those in greatest need. On many occasions during our three-and-a-half years in Rio Negro, church members would address me as 'Pastor Roy.' As Roy was a good friend of mine, I didn't mind this. We were reminded on numerous occasions of what Pastor Roy had done in the church, and if I came up with a new idea, inevitably Pastor Roy had done it before.

One evening, I was playing football with some local youngsters on a rough and sloping piece of land close to our house. As I was running for the ball, I slipped and fell, and as I did my right foot became trapped under the weight of my body. My foot was suddenly in the wrong place.

The mother of one of the boys sent him to our house to tell Maria. As she was pregnant with our second child, the mother said to be gentle in breaking this news. So, he rang the bell and when Maria opened the door, said straight out, 'Your husband's broken his leg!'

So, she came to collect me and take me to the local hospital, sitting in the front seat of our car. I can remember staring at my foot and thinking if it was possible to walk on a foot angled like mine was. While we waited for the doctor to arrive, I asked Maria if she could make my foot more comfortable. It was then that it began to really hurt. She said afterwards that she didn't even want to look, as the sight was so grotesque. I was fortunate to receive excellent care, though the sight of my right foot caused even the nurse at reception to put her hands over her face.

That evening two doctors came and reset my foot, by placing my lower right leg in some kind of tube, and then pulling my foot and turning it until it was in the correct position again. They did say that if I couldn't stand the pain, they would stop. I think that by then the pain was so intense that a little more pain made no difference. They managed to get it in place at the first attempt, though as they did so, it felt like my foot and leg were joined by elastic. I then had an x-ray which showed that my ankle was also broken. I don't know if I broke it when I fell, or whether the doctors broke it while fixing it. Anyway, I was sent home for the night. Next day back at the hospital, I was wheeled into the operating theatre at seven in the morning, and given a local anaesthetic into the spine as I sat on the side of the operating table. After what seemed to be only a few minutes, I woke up. I was lying down, and the anaesthetist was looking over me. I asked him if the operation was finished. He replied that they still hadn't begun and that I had fainted. While still conscious I heard the sound of a drill and other things but felt no pain as the surgeon worked to insert a pin into my ankle. Fortunately, the anaesthetist offered me some mild sedation to make me feel better about the whole episode. The point of sharing this story is that one caring lady from the church, who had really been as a mother to us, greeted me, after my operation, with the words: 'Oh, Pastor Roy broke his leg, too!' What could I do that Pastor Roy hadn't already done! I was fortunate, though, because someone told me later that there were two orthopaedic surgeons at the hospital, and whenever the other surgeon operated, patients always left with one leg shorter than the other!

Hop along Cassidy!
During the time my leg was in plaster, a member of our church became very ill. She was hospitalised, and a day after our last visit to her she sadly died. The funeral took place at our Baptist church, and I remember hopping towards the pulpit in order to begin the service. Fortunately, the proceedings were concluded without any mishap, though I remember a nurse from the hospital, who attended the service,

commenting that I had been a very impatient patient while under her care. Well, I do remember trying to leave the hospital on the second night in extreme pain from my right foot, which had been operated on the previous day. I remember asking for stronger painkillers, which were not forthcoming, and with my pregnant wife lying on a couch beside me, I insisted that she needed to get home to a proper bed and that I might as well go with her. Not surprisingly, that argument was summarily rejected by the attending nurse. At the cemetery, it was quite a balancing act weaving between the graves on one foot, but fortunately, I managed not to fall in during the committal at the graveside. I wasn't told whether Pastor Roy had ever done that!

To catch a thief

Another story from Rio Negro would be hilarious if it weren't also sad. One day, a young man came to our front door offering us three rolls of photographic film. We had never met the young man before, but he had heard from the local photographic shop that I used large format roll film, which is what he had with him. 'Oh, yes,' I exclaimed, 'that's just the kind of film I use, but it can't be bought in Brazil.' As it so happened, I was expecting that exact film in that exact quantity at that exact moment in the post, as I had asked a family member to send it to me. I told the boy that I would take one of the rolls of film. The arrival of this film on my doorstep left me more than a little curious. So as the young man explained to me that the local photographic shop had told him that I used this film, I went down to the shop to share the story. The young man had gone into the shop thinking that they might buy the film from him, but the owner said that he didn't use that format, but that I did. During my conversation with the owner of the photo shop, it turned out that the boy worked at the local post office. The pieces of the jigsaw were falling into place, and a more precise picture was beginning to emerge. So off we went to the post office where we related the whole story to the manager. The sad truth is the boy who worked in the backroom of the post office, sorting through the mail for distribution had his eye drawn to a package from the United Kingdom. He concluded that it must be of some value to be sent all that way to the Brazilian outpost of Rio Negro. So, he opened the package. We declined to make a formal complaint but asked for our film to be returned, which it duly was the following day.

Chapter Six

Light in our darkness

Our time in the southern town of Rio Negro was one of personal highs and lows. Our second child, Jonathan Mario, was born on 28th March 1985. Our joy at his birth was turned to heartache 24 hours later when he died from a heart disorder. He had been in an incubator, except for when a nurse brought him to Maria for feeding. The doctor was a heart specialist, though not a paediatrician. The baby was x-rayed at the main hospital in town and then put on medication overnight. I knelt by Maria's bedside and prayed to God to heal our son. By early morning his condition had suddenly deteriorated. We made immediate arrangements, with the doctor's consent, to have the baby transferred to the *Pequeno Príncipe* Children's Hospital in Curitiba. An American missionary pilot was already on his way to Rio Negro, but our baby died even before the plane arrived. We were utterly distraught.

Words cannot describe the pain we felt. But once more God was at the very centre of our grief; we knew his presence was real, even if we could not feel it because of emotional numbness. He spoke to us on the occasion we lost our baby daughter through words that we ourselves had spoken. He spoke on this occasion, too, through a dream that same evening. Our friend and senior missionary, David Doonan and his wife Doris, had flown immediately from Campo Grande, where they had been visiting colleagues. Though I wanted to stay at the hospital with Maria following her Caesarean Section, I was persuaded to go back to the house of Major Dutra and his wife who was a medical doctor. We shall meet Major Dutra and his wife again in this chapter. A meal was offered, and we all sat down at the dining room table. If I did eat anything, I don't remember. I certainly had no appetite for food. I think the rest of the company realised I was in a world apart. It was suggested that I lay down in an adjoining bedroom. I was given something to drink and then slept for a while. During my sleep, I recall I had a dream in which the sun rose in the black of night. The darkness remained all around, but the sun was shining in the blackness of space. When I awoke, I remembered the dream, unlike most dreams which are already forgotten or soon forgotten. I shall never forget that dream. It stood for me as a sign that God was present in the darkness. Strangely, it did not take the darkness away, but God was there nonetheless. That is the way the sun shines beyond the earth's atmosphere. The impenetrable blackness remains, but the light of the sun is there. Light is only seen as it is reflected from something else. I remember learning that from a science teacher at school. So where was I in my dream? I don't know. But God was with me. That dream has helped me through, and still helps me when I recall that terrible situation, even today.

We had imagined we would be taking our little boy to church on Easter Sunday morning to be dedicated to the Lord. Instead, we went without him, but in words, we cannot explain, the joy of knowing Christ, and that he had risen from the dead, filled the empty aching void of losing both our children. As I had prayed over that child in an Amazon village five years before, so I knelt beside my wife's bed and prayed to God for our own son. Do not think that God did not answer that prayer; he did. But sometimes he says, 'No.' When this happens, his purpose is not to deny us our dearest wish; it happens because he can see the end from the beginning, and knows the answer to all our 'whys?'

A cremation service was held in São Paulo, to which Maria's mother and father came. David Doonan led the service. Our colleagues Avelino Ferreira and David Grainger were also there by our side. The following year, on our return to England, we interred our baby son's ashes in the same grave as his older sister. Our good friend, Canon Norman Mantle, Vicar of the village church of St. Paul, led the committal, attended by our parents. The two occasions we were gathered in that quiet corner of the Kent countryside, were profoundly personal, and sorrow was etched on our hearts. We once again chose the most private of farewells.

A heart to make Christ known
The Rio Negro church was our family in Brazil. They were the ones we turned to in our sorrow, and they were the ones with whom we shared our deepest joy. Our three-and-a-half years of ministry in Rio Negro

were years of consolidation for the church. Some years before, the church had seen a group of more charismatic members leave the fellowship. The church slowly recovered from this experience, but healing takes time. A unique experience to us in Brazil was the absence of baptisms in the Rio Negro church. This may have been the result of the division, which was a painful experience for all concerned. Conversions take place in healthy churches. The Holy Spirit needs freedom to access the church and bring about his purposes. There were, however, many positives. The church took the bold step (the initiative of one of our young people) to organise a concert at the local sports stadium and to invite the nationally known evangelical singer, Luiz de Carvalho, to give a performance on the Saturday evening, and also in the church on the Sunday. Invitations were sent out to the other churches in the town and posters were placed inside buses and local shops.

The weekend was a great success, and several people professed their faith in Jesus Christ. Paulo Lazarino, whose idea it was to invite Luiz de Carvalho, is today a successful Baptist minister. He was the second of our young people from that church to enter the Christian ministry. The first was Jairo, who we shall meet shortly.

The Rio Negro church had a heart to make Christ known. The population of the region, in general, was Roman Catholic. Our near neighbours, who became some of our best friends, were also Catholic. Every Christmas these good Catholic families would hold a *novena.* These were small prayer gatherings in one another's homes. These lasted, as the name suggests, for nine consecutive days. A small statue of the Virgin Mary would be carried from house to house. One of my neighbours was staunchly Catholic, so I discovered to my surprise. While visiting her home, I noticed the small statue of the Virgin Mary on her coffee table. I mentioned casually that as Baptists we didn't have statues of the saints or the Virgin Mary. When she answered that she would look after her religion and that I should look after mine, I knew immediately to say no more about the subject.

Another of my neighbours, Antonio, read his Bible and had a good knowledge of its contents. He once told me that he went along with the trappings of the Church because he was a good Catholic. However, he also studied his Bible and sought to follow its teachings. He held a good position in the local Catholic Church, as a lay reader, and was assiduous in his attendance at Mass. We developed a strong friendship, and I sought to witness to him through that friendship and the opportunities it brought.

We knew that many of our neighbours in Rio Negro would not come to a Bible study or to a meeting where hymns or songs were sung. We would knock on their doors, and say that we were going to have a prayer meeting that evening in a house nearby. We invited them to join us but said if they were unable to come, we should still like to include any request they might have for prayer. I cannot remember anyone not having a prayer request. Our purpose was to build meaningful spiritual bridges with our neighbours, with whom we already enjoyed excellent relationships.

God of miracles

Jairo Alves was a bright young man and the leader of our young people. He had received a Christian upbringing by his mother and had finished his two years' conscription in the Brazilian army. During that period, he was stationed at the local barracks in Rio Negro which was the armoured tank division. One of his senior officers was Major Dutra, who with his wife, a practising doctor, attended our church. Jairo loved the army and had decided to make a career of it, and was soon to be promoted to corporal. During a game of volleyball at the barracks, he suffered the impact of a ball, which hit him in a painful spot below the waist. Sometime later, he was diagnosed with testicular cancer and underwent surgery at the military hospital in Curitiba, the state capital. Unfortunately, the cancer came back and had spread to other parts of his body. He underwent further major surgery at the Erasto Gertner Cancer Hospital in Curitiba.

On the day of his surgery, at seven in the morning, the hour he was due to go down to the operating theatre, the church gathered for prayer. It was still dark when we arrived at the church, symbolic of another kind of darkness that surrounded Jairo at that moment in time. We could only have imagined what God had in mind for this young man, but we prayed for the success of the surgery and Jairo's complete healing.

The outcome was that the doctors had cut away as much as they could, but the prognosis was far from good. The doctor from our church confided in me that according to medical opinion, Jairo had two years to live. He started chemotherapy, but this made him so ill that he refused to continue with any more treatment after the initial sessions. His life was very much in God's hands.

Following the surgery and still in his hospital bed with countless different tubes going in and out of his young body, Jairo spoke to me, saying that if the Lord spared his life, he would become a full-time pastor. Nothing more was said about this for about two years. When it could be seen that Jairo was by then in robust health again, I ventured to remind him of the vow he had made before God from that hospital bed. There was no need to persuade Jairo to keep to his part of the bargain. He applied to the Baptist Seminary in Curitiba, was accepted and did his theological training to become a Baptist minister. Jairo was given two years to live in October 1985, and today, over 30 years later, he continues to serve God through the Baptist church. I had the privilege of conducting his wedding to Leonezia in December 1991. Jairo and Leonezia have served the Lord, not only in Brazil but also as missionaries in South Africa, through the Brazilian Baptist World Missions Board. Recently, Jairo wrote to me to say that they would shortly be celebrating their 25th wedding anniversary. They have an adopted daughter, Letícia, now an attractive young woman.

The lesson and the blessing of this story are that God never gives up on us and can bring us through the darkest hours of our lives. He is also the God who answers prayer and who has power and authority over every human circumstance. Our response should be unending gratitude and praise. We have witnessed miracles in Brazil from the young child in the Amazon rainforest to this young man in one of Brazil's most developed cities. From north to south, we have seen it with our own eyes and heard it with our own ears. God is very much at work in Brazil.

What kind of spirit is this?

Here are two contrasting stories that presented challenges to our imagination and creative thinking. One day I was asked to visit the home of a member of our Baptist congregation in Roseira. The lady was concerned that her son might be possessed by an evil spirit. She asked me to visit and pray for him. This I willingly did. The question was whether the boy was suffering from demon possession or some kind of psychological disorder? Drawing on an experience from the church in Vilhena, I read from the Gospel of John, Chapter 10, concerning the Good Shepherd. One evening, in Vilhena, I was reading from the Gospel of

106

John, Chapter 10, when a commotion began among the congregation. A lady visitor had become highly agitated and made it difficult to continue with the service. Fortunately, the pastor who had been invited to preach was also the pastor of our mother church in São Paulo. He was a wise and experienced Brazilian Baptist pastor. He rose and asked the church leaders to accompany this person to a place outside the sanctuary and to pray for her deliverance. We could hear the prayers of that small group going up to heaven. A few moments later we all heard loud, high-pitched demonic cries; then silence. She had been delivered from her tormentor and was able to rejoin the congregation. As I read to this mother and her son in Roseira, I waited for a possible reaction. Usually, demons will react to the name of Jesus. In this case, there was no reaction. I concluded that the boy was not possessed of anything other than, perhaps, a problematic disposition towards his mother.

An unusual burial

The next story is also from Roseira. One day I had the privilege of conducting the funeral service of one of our church members. He was a well-loved member of our church. As is the custom at Brazilian funerals, the open coffin is brought into the building as friends and family gather round. This may go on all night depending on the hour arranged for the burial. On this occasion, the service was held in the evening and the burial the following morning. I returned to the church at eight in the morning to do the committal at a nearby cemetery.

When I arrived at the church, a member of the family approached me to say that there was some doubt as to whether their loved one was in fact dead. Apparently, the body was still warm. They asked to call a doctor to ascertain whether or not this person had, in fact, died. I naturally consented, and we waited until the doctor had examined the body and declared that death had occurred. With that, we went to the cemetery. As the coffin was being prepared to be lowered into the ground, I noticed the bones of a previous occupant. In Brazil, unkept graves are often reused, and sometimes the bones of previous occupiers are taken out. In this case, they definitely remained inside. Once the soil was replaced, they would suffer no further disturbance.

Chapter Seven

The best thing that ever happened to us

Two and a half years after the birth of Jonathan Mario, another son, João Marcos, was born to us. We had made plans for his birth to happen in Curitiba, about 65 miles to the north. Avelino and Ana Ferreira, our BMS colleagues and a much-loved missionary couple, had prepared a room in their flat for Maria and the baby. When news reached them that our baby had arrived, before we could get to Curitiba, Ana exclaimed: 'But, Maria, I've prepared the room, and everything is ready for you here!' What could we do? This baby decided to come a month early, as with the previous two pregnancies. Once again, the birth was in Rio Negro, at the same hospital, and delivered by the same Brazilian doctor. Our joy was finally restored, and though JM could never take the place of his older brother and sister, he has filled the space they left in our lives. Four months later, we moved from Rio Negro to a new location on the coastal strip of Paraná.

Someone's at the gate

It was a warm sunny February afternoon. There was a call from our front gate, and through the open window, we could see a young boy selling his catch of prawns. These had been caught in the sea locally, and we were delighted to buy some from him. We sat down at table that evening to a delicious prawn salad. So, was this a taste of things to come; our new life, set between glorious mountains and the sparkling sea? The colourful and historic town of Antonina nestles between the tree-covered *Serra do Mar* and the Bay of Paranaguá. It is little changed from 16th century colonial days. Brazil was discovered by the Portuguese in April 1500, and Antonina was first populated one-hundred-and-fifty years later.

The local people derive their living from fishing and subsistence farming. The port of Antonina, which fell into virtual disuse in the 1990s, has now reopened further out towards the sea at Ponta do Felix. It now serves as an important source of employment for the local population.

Being geographically central to the littoral of Paraná, Antonina was the strategic choice for our work in this coastal region.

Beauty is in the eye of the beholder

Our work involved giving pastoral oversight to the Baptist church which was located close to the port and there was also a small, sandy beach. The beach attracted weekend and holiday visitors to the area. Antonina was in need of a makeover as many buildings, beautiful as they were structurally and dating back to colonial days, required a coat of paint and some tender loving care. The minister of our home church in the United Kingdom came to visit us and, one day, while he and his wife were with us, commented that only God could give us a love for a town like Antonina. And he was not the only person to feel that way about Antonina. Marcelo, the young son of Antonio from Rio Negro, came to visit as well. When he first set eyes on the place, he remarked that it looked like it was falling down! Well, love Antonina we did! The church was located between the *Serra do Mar* and the South Atlantic Ocean. It was, in fact, situated on a quiet inlet of the Bay of Paranaguá. In the afternoons, though, the onshore winds would transform the peaceful waters into choppy seas.

Antonina was a fascinating place and, for many, a retreat from the busy capital at weekends. Often, we would visit a family who owned a small holding in the hills to the front of the church. We watched as the women ground manioc into flour, and the head of the house panned optimistically for gold in a nearby stream. By the roadside, at the foot of the hills, a neighbour put out a receptacle by the garden gate, containing sugar water. The sweetened water attracted many colourful hummingbirds, as we stood mesmerised watching them hover; their wings beating at around fifty times a second.

Sheep without a shepherd

We also had oversight of several small rural churches in the hinterland between the mountains and the sea. The view of the mountains from our house was breath-taking, and it was in that direction that we often travelled to attend the several churches that happened to be without a pastor. Access was along the dirt road to the colonial town of Guaraqueçaba. This town is situated on the Bay of Paranaguá and is the oldest town in Paraná, dating back to the 1500s. Thirty miles along this undulating, bumpy road, was the settlement of Potinga. This modest settlement boasted a school and a Baptist church, both situated on the main road. It was surrounded by farmland and banana plantations. BMS had a farming project in Potinga. Our colleagues, Frank and Peggy Gouthwaite, and David and Joyce Stockley worked there. The purpose of the project was to help local farmers with sustainable farming techniques. They were also encouraged to join forces and form a Cooperative for the distribution and marketing of their produce. Bananas, in particular, grew in abundance on the littoral, and their successful marketing was important for the livelihood of the local people.

Another colleague, Mary Parsons, who was a nurse, worked at the Good Samaritan Dispensary in the next village further along the road. The Dispensary provided free medical and pre-natal facilities for the local population and was supported by the Baptist churches from the state of Paraná.

It was a privilege to be part of this team. As coordinator of the Littoral Baptist Association, I visited the churches without a pastor, taking Sunday services, leading Bible studies and dropping in at their small holdings for a welcome *cafezinho*. This expression of holistic ministry was vital in a region of extensive poverty and geographic isolation.

Many tears

One Sunday morning, I received a telephone call to say that a ten-year-old girl from the Serra Negra church had died suddenly. She had been taken to hospital in Guaraqueçaba the previous evening with acute pneumonia. The doctors had wrestled with the situation all night but to no avail. This news came as a great shock, as I knew the girl and her family well. She had a lovely outgoing personality. It took me one and a half hours to drive to the church. When I arrived, there were people gathered at the door of the house of her grandparents. As I stepped inside their home, there were many tears, including my own. My own daughter had been delivered stillborn on that same October day seven years before.

The service was held in the small country church that same evening. The following morning, we went to the cemetery on a hillside outside the village. Those emotionally stretched moments were made even more challenging as the grave was too small to receive the coffin. So we all waited while more earth was removed to allow the coffin to fit in. But where do we find God in these moments? There are really no words that seem adequate, and in Brazil there is much suffering. As in our own personal experience of losing a child, it is in the presence, not the absence of suffering that we find God. That is the message of the Cross.

Painful insect bites

I would visit the islands in the Bay of Paranaguá with the assistance of local fishermen, who knew the waters well and provided the necessary and only transport available. With their help, I was able to visit the even more isolated island communities, such as Ilha Rasa, Medeiros, and the island of Superaguí, which bravely faces the wild South Atlantic Ocean. On these visits, the conditions were primitive; outside or non-existent loos, but worst of all, persistent biting insects. It caused much laughter on Ilha Rasa one evening when I sat on a wooden chair with my feet in a basin of water. I was trying to soothe the bites I had already received, only to be bitten again on the back of the neck. With a self-inflicting slap of the hand and a cry of anguish, my hosts looked on with unperturbed amusement.

All change!

When we began our visits to these churches, the members of the Serra Negra church had not taken communion for about a year. When we asked why this was, the local leader responded that no pastor had been available to preside at the communion table. In Brazilian Baptist churches, only an ordained pastor is allowed to preside at the communion service and to conduct baptisms. Serra Negra and other neighbouring churches were led by local leaders and though spiritually qualified to teach and preach they had received no formal instruction. It was not long before we realised that our priority should be to help change this situation. This we did by starting a lay training course based in Antonina. This attracted church leaders from the whole littoral region. The course was run over a period of two years and meetings were held fortnightly on a Saturday. The day was structured around study, worship, lunch, with free time after lunch. A devotional service was held before the afternoon session. There were two lessons in the morning and two in the afternoon of an hour and twenty minutes each. The students took it in turns to lead devotions and bring a short exposition from God's word. Meals were prepared by the ladies from the two Baptist churches in Antonina, and they did so with great enthusiasm and dedication. Maria was the course secretary to whom everyone would turn for one reason or another. She also bought the food we needed for lunch and generally made sure everyone was on-board. Our little son, who was always present, was adopted by the students as their mascot! There was a great atmosphere on those Saturdays. We were also greatly blessed by the support of the First Baptist Church in Antonina and their pastor, Joel dos Prazeres. Pastor Joel was a key figure in writing up the documents required for the elaboration of the Project. These were presented to the Littoral Baptist Association for their approval, which was duly given. The result was the mobilisation of the churches and the blessing of God.

Pastors of the local churches, which enjoyed pastoral oversight, helped teach the material from interactive study books obtained from the São Paulo state

Baptist Convention. The fortnightly meetings turned out to be not only a time of serious study but also of rich fellowship. To be able to bring together representatives of most of our churches on a regular basis was an inspiration and encouragement to all those involved in this venture.

We invested in people and their local churches. My own work in Brazil and its value to God's kingdom should always be measured by the outcome for those we have been privileged to serve. Sometimes our own success appeared to be diminished by the lack of progress once we had left a project. But fruits had been gathered in for the glory of God, and this was reward enough. A senior colleague once said that many things were achieved in Brazil by BMS missionaries that otherwise, humanly speaking, would never have happened without them.

Extension Course held in Antonina

A fantastic result

There was, nonetheless, considerable evidence of excellent results. At the conclusion of the first two years of the course, twelve students received their certificates in recognition of their efforts and three received special mention for their exceptional performances. The first student, a retired bank clerk, received a special commendation for the highest overall marks obtained. The second, who lived the furthest distance from Antonina, was commended for the best attendance at the course, almost one-hundred-percent. The third student gained a special prize for having made the most progress in his studies during those two years. His only daughter spoke to us sometime after, saying that since her father had started the course, he had become a better father to her and a better husband to her mother. Teaching from the Bible and teaching about spiritual leadership is not only about sharing information and facts. It also provides knowledge that leads to a closer walk with Jesus Christ and a deeper relationship with him.

Heaven be praised!

On our first Easter Sunday on the Littoral, we gathered with the church on a large rock by the water's edge. The place where we met was known as *Ponta da Pita* in Antonina. It was moments before daybreak as we gathered at this idyllic spot.

During the course of that simple service, while we were singing 'Up from the Grave He Arose', we watched as a fisherman glided past silently in his canoe, hardly making a ripple. Then, moments later, five or six dolphins bobbed in and out of the glass-like water with a gracefulness and beauty words can hardly describe. The service concluded as we embraced one another in the knowledge that Christ is our risen Lord. Twenty-five years later, Maria and I spent Easter weekend in Antonina and returned to that very spot. The church had once more gathered for a sunrise service, as they had done every Easter Sunday morning in all the intervening years. As I stood waiting for the pastor to begin the service, he came up to me and said: 'They want you to do it.' It brought a tear to my eye. Just as well I had come prepared. But I knew Brazilians well enough to have some notes in readiness for a sermon! It was such a privilege, and brought wonderful memories flooding back of the first Easter Sunday morning we had gathered there.

Didn't they do well!

One of the rewards of ministry is serving across generations of families. Even more so, the privilege of following the progress of the children of members of a congregation and watching them grow and develop and become parents themselves. When we first arrived in Antonina, we decided to visit each church family, in turn, beginning with those that lived the furthest distance from the church. As there were no road names or house numbers to help in the majority of cases, we relied on the youngsters to show us where the different families lived. Our dependence on them and the opportunity to give value to these young lives was the beginning of friendships that continue to the present day. They have now moved to larger towns in the state of Paraná, and one lives with his wife and children in Florida, in the United States. They have all come a long way from those distant childhood days.

A surprise invitation

Totally unexpectedly our Mission Leader asked us to become the hostel parents for our colleagues' children in São Paulo. Taking up this role meant leaving the tranquil backwater colonial town of Antonina and moving to the largest and busiest metropolis in South America. We made plans to relocate to São Paulo on the anniversary of my ordination, the 2nd July. In the event, this was delayed by one day. I had been asked by a local family to take the funeral of a new-born baby; a terribly sad moment to end our ministry in Antonina. This event brought back memories of our own tragic losses.

The following day, we drove the 260 miles from Antonina to São Paulo to begin our year at the BMS hostel in Vila Sônia, a suburb on the south side of the city. Our year in São Paulo brought me opportunities for further study, which might not have been possible in the context of a busy pastoral ministry. It was a window of opportunity, which ended up lasting nine years and culminated in the successful conclusion of both masters and doctoral studies. It was a time for practice and reflection to come together; this would open up new and more challenging opportunities further ahead.

Between the two of us, Maria and I were housekeeper, cook, surrogate parents, chauffeur, uncle and aunty to the seven adolescents entrusted to our care. The housework was shared with Raquel, our live-in maid from the littoral of Parana. Raquel was the daughter of one of our extension course students in Antonina (the one who gained the progress prize) and had already been working at the hostel for two years before our arrival there. Four months on, in November 1991, Brazil held its ten-yearly census. One day the doorbell rang and before us stood a lady with a clipboard and form ready to take the details of who lived at our house. As it was the school holidays, the children were away visiting their parents in distant parts of Brazil. Among the questions, we were asked were: 'How many people live permanently in this house?' Answer: 'Three.' Then we were asked, 'How many rooms does this house have?' This was followed by, 'How many bathrooms?' To this last question, we had to do some quick arithmetic, which brought the response, 'Nine!' We felt acutely embarrassed to have three bathrooms each!

Chilling out

On Saturdays, a regular practice was to spend a day with the children at the local shopping centre and ice rink, or at the theme park on the other side of the city. On one occasion, we went to a safari park on the edge of town. We would also go to the beach in Santos. Even in August, during the Brazilian winter, it was warm enough to do this.

When we visited the safari park, we saw lions, giraffes and apes close up; some apes even jumped onto the front of the car. The windows were left open, but for our safety, temporary bars were fitted by the park officials, to prevent these dangerous primates from getting inside the car and causing pandemonium among the children and adults.

Fun, tantrums and being teenagers

Mealtimes were always eventful, with some lively discussions, and usually, a question or two to test their general knowledge. These activities kept them occupied and entertained while eating their food. One mealtime ended up with a normally well-behaved child tipping her drink into my lap. A palpable silence followed, which in turn was followed by the perpetrator being summarily sent to her room. With fine mediation skills on the part of Maria, an apology was eventually forthcoming and, to my shame, only reluctantly accepted. The following day all was forgotten.

One evening two of the boys were playing darts in their bedroom. The dartboard was on the wall where it should have been, but the two boys were throwing the darts into the door, where they should not have been. Just as well that when Maria went in, they weren't throwing a dart in her direction!

The year passed, and the children all performed well at school. The support we received from the parents was exceptional. It was a privilege to serve our colleagues in this way and to forge lasting friendships with these families and their children entrusted to our care.

On the high seas

In July 1992, we set sail for home assignment in the United Kingdom. As we were close to the port of Santos, we opted for a sea voyage. The cargo vessel we boarded belonged to the Italian Grimaldi Line. It could carry seventeen passengers, and we were very well looked after. We struck up a friendship with a Danish couple who had a little girl about the same age as João Marcos. It was at the time of the Euro 92 football competition, which Denmark won for the first time in their history. You can imagine the excitement! There was no entertainment on board, but there was a swimming pool under the funnel, which spewed out black soot into the water. Needless to say, it was seldom used. There was also a cycling machine, to keep us in good shape, a library and a card room. The food was excellent. One evening squid was on the menu. Our young son seemed to enjoy it, though his parents chose to pass on that one. We were at sea for seventeen days and nights before we arrived in Tilbury. We shared the company of our Danish friends, and Australian and German nationals, one of whom was a botanist returning from *Tierra del Fuego*. They were all excellent company on that long journey.

One of the most memorable impressions of our voyage on the high seas was to observe the globe forming a perfect circle of 360 degrees as we looked round in all directions. For crossing the equator, we received a certificate from the ship's Captain at a special presentation ceremony on board. We watched as flying fish leapt out of the water in the dead calm of the Doldrums, the only time we were allowed to approach the bow of the ship. One passenger sat on the bow itself, and there was a massive hole in the floor for the anchor to pass. I made sure that João Marcos kept very close to my side the whole time.

The choppy seas around the Canary Islands were in striking contrast to the Doldrums. The rough seas were even more accentuated by the sight of small yachts being tossed up and down violently in the big swell. As we passed Tenerife to our left, we could make out volcanic Mount Teide in the distance.

We met some deep-sea fishermen far out in the Bay of Biscay, on occasion getting entangled in their nets to their great displeasure. The Bay of Biscay was, surprisingly, like a millpond in mid-July. We remember, also, the palpable blackness of night when at sea. At journey's end when we were keen to get ashore, it was frustrating to have to wait at a standstill in the muddy waters off the coast of Essex for a whole afternoon. The delay was caused by the Port of London Authority as they had to send out a pilot and tug to guide us through the narrow, deep water channel, in the Thames estuary to our destination. Finally, we were treated to a masterpiece of precision skill, as the captain of our ship, steered us into the incredibly narrow berth at Tilbury Docks; first taking the helm on one side, and then on the other, at the bow of the ship.

We arrived in Tilbury at six o'clock in the evening, on Saturday 25th July. It was, by then, too late to disembark that day, as the customs authorities had to inspect the ship before we could land. We had to sleep another night on board tied up in Tilbury Docks. The next morning, our families were waiting for us at the Marie Celeste Hotel, and from there we made our way over the new Queen Elizabeth II Bridge to Sidcup, where we were to spend the next year. Our son began his English schooling, as a rising five, at Longlands Primary School. Maria kept house, and I continued my studies towards a Master's degree in Applied Theology. During this time, we visited the churches across the country to share with them the stories of our life in Brazil.

Chapter Eight

The European South

We returned to Brazil to a new location in the south, in the state of Santa Catarina. Fourteen years earlier, we had done a tour of this state, before going to Rondônia. Santa Catarina was like a dream come true. For fourteen years we worked and waited for this moment, just as Jacob had to wait and work for fourteen years before he could take his beloved Rachel back home to meet his family.

Our first task was to find somewhere to live. After an extensive search for a house in Rio do Sul, we turned to Brusque. This small town is about an hour's drive from the coast; not that we had any previous plans to look there. Brusque is the centre of a thriving fabric industry. People would go there to buy fabrics at factory prices and sell them in their own towns. Someone known to us would travel to Brusque a few times a year and take the fabrics back to his shop in Vilhena to sell there, over twelve hundred miles away.

We soon found an apartment in the attractive gardens area of *Jardim Maluche*. This property was located within an hour of arriving there, through a local estate agent. As our work was to be state-wide, it wasn't too important where we lived, but Brusque served us well, especially for its excellent Roman Catholic School, São Luiz, in the centre of town.

The state of Santa Catarina is very European in orientation. Blumenau, for example, is a beautiful town on the banks of the river Itajaí-Açu, twenty-five miles northwest of Brusque. Every year the population, together with visitors, holds a typical German beer festival, known as *Oktoberfest*. The original reason for this was to stimulate the town's recovery, and that of its economy, after the devastating floods of 1983. Today, though, it has become more of a beer and folk festival for its own sake, and a chance to make merry.

In Brusque, the evangelical churches were granted the Feast of the Transfiguration, as a public holiday. As far as I know, this festival is not observed anywhere else in Brazil. Brusque boasted an influential Lutheran community and probably was granted this exception for political as much as religious reasons. The Lutheran community would have had considerable political clout in the town, at the very least when it came to the ballot box. But because the town already had its full quota of public holidays, local as well as national, it had to relinquish one of these. Incredibly, they chose to forego the most important public holiday of all, Independence Day. So Brusque, as far as we know, is the only town in Brazil to celebrate the Christian festival of the Transfiguration, and the only one not to commemorate the national holiday on Independence Day.

From the road that connects Brusque to the coastal highway, we could observe flooded rice fields on the northern side. When the rice crop appeared above the water, the fields turned a vivid green colour to dazzle our eyes. This kind of activity we have not seen anywhere else in Brazil. We relocated to this region of Brazil because I had been invited to oversee the Department of Theological Education of the Santa Catarina Baptist Convention. Training leaders for the churches in this state had been on the back burner for a few years. My brief was to revitalise the training and give it new direction. Training had to be within reach of the churches around the state, an area geographically the size of England and Wales combined.

Mapping the territory

Where does one begin? We followed the trail of interested churches, which took us all over the state of Santa Catarina from São José in the south to Joinville in the north; Itajaí in the east to Lages in the central highlands; and Taquaral and Curitibanos on the northern plateau. On many a night, I made my way through the hills and winding road between the towns of Brusque and São João Batista, to teach the small group of students who met there. Because deserted roads can be dangerous and unpredictable, especially after dark, this particular journey was always done with some apprehension and a touch of relief on arriving home safely.

Once a fortnight I would go to Taquaral. In winter it would be dark as I reached the mountain pass from São Bento do Sul to Corupá. This was the same road that we had taken on our tour of Santa Catarina in 1979 when it was a gravel surface. Now the surface had been paved. One clear night the fog came down as I made my way into this mountain pass. I could hardly make out the road in front of me for most of that stretch of twenty-two miles. It made for a long journey driving at about five to ten miles an hour. Fortunately, I could hug the side of the road furthest from the edge where the road dropped off into the valley below. That night I was caught by surprise and after that would not take the shortcut, but follow the main road if there was a chance of fog. Sometimes on these journeys, I was more aware of danger than on others. It is often when one least expects something to go wrong that it does. I would often give thanks to God in public and private prayer for his protection, even when nothing went wrong.

The journeys to the isolated villages of the Paraná littoral were similar. With no asphalt or road markings on the road, the dark nights called for special care and attention. On one occasion, returning at night from a church service, I misjudged a bend in the road by a precipice and was saved from disaster only by the thick vegetation growing along the roadside. After that, I always stayed overnight and travelled home the next morning. To this day, I am grateful for the hospitality of the local people; for supper and a warm bed, whenever and wherever I travelled in Brazil.

A perilous moment

On another occasion, we were returning from São Paulo to Antonina, after a Mission retreat. I could see a car behind us in my rear window. I looked again, and it was no longer there. As we were on a mountain pass with a sheer rock face to one side and no turning off at that point, I was curious as to why it had disappeared from view. I looked again, which took my attention away from the road ahead. We were going into a bend, and when I turned my attention back to the road, I had to make an abrupt adjustment to my line of travel. Our car did not respond at all well to that sudden manoeuvre and began to veer first to the right and then the left sides of the road. I held the steering wheel instinctively knowing that to try and correct my line of travel again might only make things worse. The car needed to be steadied; that was the first priority. There was really nothing I could do except stay calm in that situation. Though it seemed like an age, the car did begin to drive normally as the momentum which was dragging it from side to side abated. Eventually, it was under my control once again. Only then did I realise the grave danger we all faced. If a lorry had come in the opposite direction at any point during those 20 seconds or so, it would never have seen us on that long corner, close to the rock face, on the wrong side of the road, travelling towards it. Just then our three-year-old son, exclaimed in

Portuguese, *'Que legal!'* which when translated means, 'that was cool!' How blissfully unaware he was of the danger we had all faced. Moments later, a massive lorry passed us going in the opposite direction. Even when we didn't have time to pray, God knew our need and kept us safe.

Working together

Throughout the state, leadership courses were arranged between the local churches and the Department of Theological Education. The teaching was carried out by local pastors and myself, as Director of the Department. The course we ran moved around the state, the location depending on where requests to train church leaders came from. In this way, we were able to decentralise and democratise theological education in Santa Catarina. Over a period of six years, we trained more than two-hundred leaders for the various churches. Investing in people continues to give a good return, year in year out. To supplement the training done in local churches, we held an annual residential course at the Baptist Camp, near Florianópolis, the state capital. The course brought together students from all over the state. Where there were financial constraints, we tried to subsidise the costs of the tuition to our students, which included teaching, food and transport.

Time to build

An experienced American missionary, Wesley (Boots) Blackwell, responded to an offer from the churches of the Southern Baptist Convention, to build a theological training centre at the Baptist Camp. This paved the way for the residential school, with teaching rooms and accommodation on site. Wesley had been approached several times by the Southern Baptists with the offer of funds to build a centre for theological education and leadership training in Santa Catarina. He had declined all previous offers because of a lack of initiative regarding leadership training. He now sensed the time had come to accept that offer. Teachers from Curitiba and São Paulo accepted our invitation to teach on this annual course, and some came with their families. The beautiful setting of the Baptist Camp and Retreat Centre and its proximity to the glorious beaches of Florianópolis made it possible to combine work and leisure. The teaching timetable was devised to allow for teachers to have free time, either mornings or afternoons. The Department of Theological Education provided for the cost of transport and accommodation, together with the Santa Catarina Baptist Convention. Tragically, Wesley was killed in a road accident in Santa Catarina a year later, leaving a wife and young family. His legacy is part of our legacy in Santa Catarina.

The fruits of our labours

The results of democratising theological education have produced many church leaders and several pastors. In particular, the churches in Papanduva, Itajaí and São Francisco do Sul have benefitted from this initiative. João Pires, Everaldo Prateat and Klaus Friese have had pastoral responsibility of these churches in the state of Santa Catarina. Other churches have also been blessed by their ministry. These are some of the 'lasting fruits' that Jesus spoke about when he asked his disciples to produce fruit for the kingdom. João and Everaldo assumed the leadership of churches for which we had had pastoral responsibility. So it was an integral part of our service to these churches, to be able to train the next generation of leaders to take over from us, allowing them to carry the work forward.

So where did these young leaders come from? They were all local church members, and were known to the churches they were being prepared to lead. In Brazil, there is a sense that pastoral leadership nurtured in other churches is to be preferred. We hope that we may have helped change this attitude towards locally grown leadership. João and Everaldo initially met with resistance to their leadership, simply because they were 'sons of Joseph.' And so they experienced first-hand what Jesus experienced when he was rejected by the population in Nazareth. 'A prophet is not without honour, except among his own people.' There is an interesting and amusing story surrounding João's acceptance as evangelist in Roseira. He had agreed to take on this responsibility when, at the last minute, he had second thoughts. He had felt that the appointment had been our decision rather than that of the church. He was probably right, though it had not occurred to us that the church might have reservations. He told us that he had decided not to assume the leadership of the church. His change of mind came as a complete surprise to us and unravelled our plans to leave the church with continuing leadership. What could we do to avert this calamity?

I felt that if there was the possibility of resistance to João's leadership, it was more perceived on his part than real. An idea occurred to me. There was in the church in Roseira, a venerable gentleman, and founder member, named Donato Gonçalves. I knew that the church would listen to Brother Donato, as he was affectionately and respectfully known. I went to visit him at his home in Rio Negro and asked him if he supported the idea that João should lead the church. He responded positively, and I asked him if he would speak to the church meeting and commend João as their evangelist. To this request, he also responded positively. The next Sunday morning, following the church service, we held a business meeting, and Donato spoke to the church, recommending that João should be their evangelist. The church agreed without hesitation, dissent or discussion. João was formally appointed to be their leader and evangelist. This outcome gave João the authority he needed, and the church saw it as their appointment. Everyone was satisfied.

The leadership of both João and Everaldo was ultimately endorsed by their respective local congregations, and these two young men went on to serve their people well. João continued as the evangelist in Roseira for seven years, and Everaldo continues to serve as pastor of the church in Itajaí to this day. As we said our 'goodbyes' to the New Jerusalem Church, Everaldo turned to me and said: 'Thank you for believing in us.' That is what our ministry in Brazil has always been about; believing in people, so as they will believe in themselves. In believing in themselves, they can then contribute with all their potential to the expansion of God's kingdom. To illustrate the point, some years later, Klaus was elected President of the Santa Catarina Baptist Convention, a testimony to the high regard in which he was held within Baptist circles. When we faithfully sow seeds and care for the young plants, God will bring that growth to fruition for the praise of his glory.

Answers to prayer

Before we assumed the pastoral care of the New Jerusalem Church, we had been members of the First Baptist Church in Itajaí. You may remember that this was one of the churches we visited on our tour of Santa Catarina when we first arrived in Brazil. One evening, after the service, a young woman came up to me to describe a very distressing situation in her life. Her father had recently died, and she was having frightening dreams in which he appeared. She asked me to pray for her. As I often do when people ask for prayer, I suggested we prayed together there and then. I have even been present when a Brazilian pastor has prayed over the phone with someone in need of God's help. I have learned so much from Brazilians about being the people of God. I also believe that as British missionaries, we have been able to shape the church in Brazil. The point is that the following week this same person came to me to say that, from that moment, she no longer had any of those bad dreams.

On another occasion, an elder of the same church told me a fascinating story, and I should like to share this with you. One day a mother had requested that he pray for her son. Have we not heard that before? He said he would, but asked that she also pray for her son. So, she went away satisfied that her son would be covered by this godly man's prayers. A while later she returned to thank him for his prayers. 'Thank you for praying for my son,' she said, 'He is so much better.' The elder paused for a moment and then asked if she had prayed for her son. She told him she had done so. 'Well,' he said, 'the truth is I forgot to pray for your son; therefore, it is your prayers that God has answered.' So, this dear mother was blessed twice over.

Open our eyes, Lord
One morning I phoned the Executive Director of our state Baptist Convention. I can't remember the reason for my calling him, but I remember very well the conversation that took place. He had received the annual returns from the churches; this included the number of baptisms in each church. He was disappointed that only five-hundred baptisms had

occurred during the previous calendar year. Now, before I go on, I should put you in the picture with regard to Baptist work in this southern Brazilian state. Santa Catarina has a predominantly German population. The Lutheran church in this state is strong, or at least, the state has a solid Lutheran tradition. The strength of the Lutheran Church was, in part, the reason for the relatively small impact that Baptists had made over the previous one-hundred years since Baptist work began in that state. It was considered to be the one state in Brazil where Baptist work had struggled to make a significant impact. When I heard our Executive Director giving his view on the statistics before him, I thought for a moment. Our total Baptist church membership in the state, at that time, was four-thousand. This was the current total of Baptists after one-hundred years of involvement in the state. I drew our Executive Director's attention to the fact that five-hundred baptisms in a single year was an excellent result if one compared the figures against the church growth over the previous one-hundred years. If that kind of growth were replicated over the next one-hundred years, Baptist strength in the state would be fifty-thousand members, compared with three-thousand over the previous century. Well, this was truly a revelation for our Executive Director. From that moment on, he went around the churches telling them how well they were doing and how the tide had turned for the Baptist churches in the state of Santa Catarina. The astonishing truth is that there was a higher rate of growth in church membership in our state that year (13%) than in any other state in Brazil. For me, this was a truly significant moment. We had been privileged to be part of a unique event in the life of the Brazilian Baptist Church. God was at work, even in Santa Catarina. In fact, especially in Santa Catarina!

Difficulties ahead

Taking leave of our friends and students in January 2000 was made a little easier by the excitement of another challenge ahead. To date, our work in Brazil had presented both of us with many challenges, and we had thoroughly enjoyed our time there. Many years ago, soon after our arrival in Brazil, a friend from our home church in London wrote to us. He was pleased that we were settling down well and that we were excited about the future work. He also suggested that we might feel differently once the novelty had worn off. Well, the novelty may have diminished, but our love for Brazil certainly hadn't. We took our leave of the students who had gathered to say goodbye at the Baptist Camp during their third residential training week. We were pleased to be able to leave the work we had begun in the capable hands of our successor, Pastor Francisco, a retired military officer. We had felt that it was better to hand over a ship in good order and moving ahead at full steam, rather than when everything had been done and there were no challenges left. Though the vision for leadership training has been taken forward in different formats, the Project we had begun and nurtured was not followed through as we had hoped it would be. In his first and last report a year later, Pastor Francisco concluded that the goodwill that we had enjoyed on the part of the students and teachers was not transferable. His remarks suggested that he did not have the necessary support for his plans for the Project.

Finding a solution

Others took over the leadership of the Project on a yearly basis for the next couple of years, but they were not able to progress the Project in the way we had envisaged. Our attempts to secure a conclusion to the studies of existing students were to no avail. Finally, in 2004, we were able to present certificates to the students in Santa Catarina, though not in the name of the Santa Catarina Baptist Convention. This was done in the name of our newly formed Seminary in Natal, in northeast Brazil. So eventually, recognition was given to those who had pursued their studies with sacrifice and exemplary dedication. The service in Joinville was held with the knowledge and support of the Executive Director of the Santa Catarina Baptist Convention. This position had changed hands since we left the state. The graduation service was led by the Executive Secretary of the state's Northern Baptist Association at the Living Stones Baptist Church. I had the privilege of preaching at that service and presenting the certificates to the deserving students.

Our journey north

The long trip to Natal was supposed to be undertaken by plane; however, we decided to see more of the country and travel by road. Maria and I with our son set off from the Baptist Camp at a mid-point along the beautiful coast of Santa Catarina. We had been holding our third annual residential course for church leaders. We were two adults, one child and two dogs.

On the first day of our journey to São Paulo, we stayed overnight at the mission hostel. As it was the summer holidays in Brazil, the children were not in residence. This visit brought back memories of our time there as hostel parents; strange in a way as both we and the hostel had moved on. The studies that I had begun there were coming to fruition with the approaching completion of my doctoral thesis on grassroots theological education. My thesis covered our periods of service in Paraná and Santa Catarina. The next morning, we set off for the emerald green hills of Minas Gerais state. We had planned our overnight stops in advance, and we aimed to travel for about eight hours a day. We phoned all the hotels where we wanted to stay, and, incredibly, only one would not accept our two dogs.

Each day we made regular stops at two-hourly intervals and with a small dose of Valium for the dogs (recommended by the vet), we made it from one hotel to the next. We mainly followed the inland BR 116, until we turned off to connect with the coastal road again. We had begun our journey in the far south on this road and had to pass through nine Brazilian states. It was a journey of nearly 2,300 miles or the distance between London and Athens.

Each state we passed through gave us a different experience. The tree-covered mountains of the southern states; the urban sprawl of the city of São Paulo; the green hills of Minas Gerais; the barren scenery and poorly kept roads of Bahia (which presented a stark and unexpected contrast, as we crossed the border of these two states). And then, as we progressed further into our journey, the magnificent sugar cane plantations of the northeast coastal region. The last stretch of the journey began with a refuelling stop at the turning leading to Baía Formosa, in Rio Grande do Norte. We were still about two hours from our destination in Natal. As we drove off the wide forecourt and onto the main highway, the undulating road stretched out before us as far as the eye could see. Our twelve-year-old son exclaimed, 'It's going to be a long two hours!'

It was the sugar cane harvest, and trundling up and down the road were huge 'trains' carrying the canes that had been first burned and then cut down from the many plantations in the region. The sugar cane trains are like iron cages on wheels. Usually, three or more joined together and driven by a motorised vehicle at the front. We often saw the sugar cane workers in their colourful, protective clothing, sometimes waiting for their own transport home, or being driven in lorry loads from the plantations down to the main road to catch their bus. This last leg of our journey to Natal did take us a little longer than two hours, but we finally arrived in the city, dusty and tired, half-an-hour before nightfall. We drove into the grounds of our newly rented accommodation, a large single storey house, and let the two dogs out of the car. They ran and jumped euphorically – high in spirits, as well as Valium. Our next adventure was about to begin.

Chapter Nine

Our remarkable son

Moving house and location, though exciting, does have its downside. For us parents, the transition is nearly always smooth. For an adolescent child, following his parents in their desire to serve God, there are additional challenges; a new school, new friendships as yet unformed, and, worst of all, old friends that are left behind. For Maria and me, leaving one church behind and walking into another is relatively straightforward. But that's only half the story. We soon make new friends, and our new church is there to meet us with open arms. We come as God's servants with a story to tell, and our new church friends are always eager to get to know us. And even where there is reticence towards the stranger, barriers soon melt away or fall down as we get to know one another.

For our young son, moving on with his parents is like starting over from scratch again. The moving didn't get easier for him. The truth is, it becomes more difficult with each move. For João Marcos, our transfer to Natal was his third and, until then, no sooner had he settled down with a new school and friends, it was time to move on again, or so it seemed. He only complained once, and this was after the move to Natal. But he won through and made some excellent friends with whom he keeps in touch to the present day.

Five hundred years of history at our feet

In January 2002, we met with other colleagues for our annual retreat at the Iguassu Falls on the frontier with Argentina. After the retreat we decided to return to Natal by road, not in our car this time but on an interstate bus. We stopped over in the interior of São Paulo state, before going on to Porto Seguro in Bahia. Porto Seguro is a place of special significance for Brazil. It was here that Brazil was discovered by Pedro Álvares Cabral, the Portuguese maritime explorer. We stood on the beach where a cross has been erected; the exact spot where Cabral and his crew celebrated the first act of Christian worship in that land. We continued our journey to Maceió, on

Porto Seguro – Site of first act of
Christian worship in Brazil

the coast further north. Northeast fishermen go out to sea in *jangadas*, wooden rafts powered by a single, triangular sail. We discovered that local fishermen would take tourists on one of these rudimentary fishing vessels and sail out to a sandbank. We didn't venture out as far as the courageous, native fishermen, though we did venture out further than usual for us. We swam in the warm azure waters of this tropical sea. Paradise!

The Divine nudge

It was at this stage of his life that our son João Marcos began home-schooling in preparation for his O Levels. It wasn't our plan that he should homeschool, but this came about during his second bout of dengue fever in June 2001. It was at the time of his half-yearly school exams. The doctor had said that João Marcos could sit his exams, but not go in for normal lessons, as this would prove too taxing for him, given the debilitating effects of dengue fever. Though he was over the worst, he was still not well enough to go to school. On the day of his first exam, I went with him and spoke with one of the school coordinators.

Unfortunately, the person responsible for João Marcos's year was away that day. The person I did speak to was quite intransigent and insisted that unless João Marcos attended standard lessons, he couldn't sit his exams. I was told that it would be possible for him to sit all the exams the following week when normal lessons had finished. However, that would not have given our son sufficient time to recover his physical strength and powers of concentration. He would have to be able to sit all his exams, one after the other. This option was normally for pupils who had failed in one or more subjects and needed to re-sit those particular exams. In Brazilian schools, if a student failed or missed even one exam, they would have to repeat that entire school year. So, we were between a rock and a hard place. That might not have been a totally impossible situation. We could have simply accepted that he would have to do the exams the following week, which in the end is what happened. For my meeting with the school staff, I had taken with me a letter from the doctor asking that our son be excused normal classes. He had also written that he would be well enough to sit his exams. The school coordinator then began to explain to me that usually these doctors' letters were fakes and that he would not accept this one from our doctor.

We returned home, by which time I had already decided that João Marcos should now study for his GCE O levels at home, and not continue with his Brazilian education beyond the end of that academic year. With hindsight, this turned out to be the best thing that could have happened regarding his future education. He wasn't able to do the same exams as he would have sat in England under the GCSE system, as these were based on coursework, as well as written papers. So he did the old-fashioned 'O levels', which he sat at the British Council in Recife. To his credit, he passed in all six subjects, with good grades, including English and Maths. There is such a thing as the 'Divine nudge', which I have felt on occasions. We needed that nudge to make us take the right decision, educationally, for our son to have the best chance of going to a British university and getting a good job at the end of it. We had no intention of ending his Brazilian schooling when I took our son to school that day. But it would have been the wrong preparation for his future had he stayed where he was.

Towards the end of his O level studies, God unexpectedly opened the way for JM to study for his A Levels in England. St George's School, in Hertfordshire, is an excellent co-educational school with a big reputation. But leaving JM in a place that none of us had known before was the most significant challenge of all our lives. I accompanied him for the school interview, which was required of prospective boarders. We travelled to London from Brazil. The headmaster, since retired, gave us a warm welcome and we were able to see the boarding school and meet the boarding master, with whom we are still good friends. JM was pleased to be accepted as a future student of the school. We returned to Brazil and then within a few months were back in England ready for this new chapter in our lives. That summer we enjoyed a family holiday in Dumfries and Galloway, in Scotland. We wanted to spend that time together before the next and very different phase of our lives. The culture shock of boarding and homesickness were the primary difficulties to be faced by JM. For his parents, who returned to their work in Brazil, it was to be without the important third member of the family, who had always been there, to take to school and fetch from school. His constant chatter around the house, his smiling face, and his precious presence are things that we missed more than words can say.

We counted the days and weeks and months between his visits to us. Thankfully, the experience was the making of him. We saw how he matured as a young adult; his appointment as Head Boy of Boarding at St. George's and the esteem in which he was held by his peers and superiors was significant reward. We are very proud of our son, of what he has achieved and the way he faced and scaled the mountain before him.

For the disadvantaged

Our work in Natal, like previous assignments, since our time on the littoral of Paraná, focused on theological education and leadership training. Our aim was to break the mould of theological education in Brazil, which traditionally was the preserve of the elite (those who could afford it and had the necessary academic qualification to work towards a Bachelor's degree). Our desire was that theological education should be for all God's people.

I believe that the whole church should be theologically literate and that the local church is the primary place for doing theology (by 'doing theology' I mean engaging in reflective practice or *praxis*). We saw our mission to Brazil as primarily for the disadvantaged, economically, socially or educationally. Many of our students had simply

147

lacked the opportunity to further their studies or improve life for themselves and their families. We aimed to provide that opportunity for those who were willing to accept it. It was sufficient reward to see the church grow through the dedicated efforts of our students of all ages and both sexes, from north to south of that great country.

Not every church member is called to be a theologian. Not every church member is called to be a pastor or missionary, or teacher. But all are called to give an account of their faith and to explain in basic, simple terms why they are followers of Jesus. We, as a couple, were called by God to serve the kingdom of God among the disadvantaged people of Brazil. Those who were left behind, as a result of a lack of opportunity, rather than their potential, could now aspire to a role of leadership, no longer just pew fodder in a Brazilian Baptist church.

Before our arrival in Natal, we had, as a family, made a reconnaissance visit there. We had also visited the state of Piauí, which is also in northeast Brazil. Of these two places, Natal seemed to offer the better opportunity for developing our vision of leadership training. The leaders of the Rio Grande do Norte Baptist Convention arranged a meeting with their Department of Theological Education. They presented us with an outline of the current situation and what they saw as the scope for its future development. Following this meeting, I received a formal invitation to move from southern Brazil to take up the challenge of developing a training programme for this state. This work would build on our previous experience, but also give us the opportunity to step outside of our comfort zone.

Upwardly mobile

In the state of Rio Grande do Norte, theological education consisted of a small leadership training centre (CTL). We had been asked to oversee the work carried out by the Centre and also to develop lay training throughout the state.

We were able to leave the day to day running of the centre in Natal in the capable hands of a Brazilian educator. We focused our efforts initially on taking to the churches of this state, the principles of theological education we had used in Santa Catarina.

Our first task was to identify locations where there was interest in running a course once a fortnight. A number of pastors came forward and invited us to visit their churches and speak with those interested in joining a class. Within a year, classes had commenced in several interior towns, including Mossoró in the northwest (the second largest town in the state), Caicó in the Seridó region (central south), and Goianinha (in the southeast). As time progressed, classes also started in Pau dos Ferros (extreme west), and Currais Novos, also in the Seridó region. We now had most of the state covered. To help you understand the geography of Rio Grande do Norte, the outline of the state boundary is in the shape of an elephant, if you view it from east to west. It is a semi-arid region of the globe, where it may not rain for years on end, creating a greyish lunar landscape. Then, occasionally, comes a year of torrential tropical rain causing widespread floods, with considerable damage to roads and bridges, homes, crops and livestock.

It was essential to some of our prospective students that our courses were recognised by the Brazilian Ministry of Education. They wished to use our courses and their successful completion as a way up the educational ladder. For others in the local churches, our courses were important as a training tool for the formation of future leaders. The fact that they were recognised or otherwise by the secular authorities was immaterial.

At the same time, there was a desire on the part of the churches in Natal for the Leaders' Training Centre to be upgraded to Seminary level. We accepted the challenge but stressed that the new Seminary would offer courses at basic and intermediate level, as well as for degree students. On 2nd August 2003, the Potiguar Theological Seminary was started. The new Seminary grew out of the former Leaders' Training Centre, rather than replaced it. The word 'Potiguar' refers to the native people of a vast swathe of the Brazilian northeast, of which Rio Grande do Norte is a part. In addition to the structure of courses, we also had to write our Constitution and fulfil government requirements, in order for the new Seminary to be recognised as a formal teaching institution. Almost immediately, the student intake increased from forty to sixty, and this number was maintained during our leadership of the Seminary.

When things are going really well, the opposition is never far away. Our end of year letter that year explains how true this is:

The year 2003 was one of the hardest we can remember on our health. We all managed to get dengue fever at different times (Maria and João Marcos for the second time). John started the year by going down with acute pancreatitis, which put him in hospital for nine days in January-February. And just when we thought it was safe to come out, in November John was hit by a car on his way to the Seminary. He was standing on the pavement waiting to cross the road when an oncoming car skidded out of control, mounted the pavement and whacked him in the middle of the back. Up, up he went onto the car, loud noises and flashing lights in his head, before he was thrown to the ground in front of the car. Miraculously the car had stopped, and he landed on his feet with only grazes to his elbows and back! All this happened in full view of Maria as she waited for him to cross the road in front of the Seminary. Soon Seminary staff and students were on the scene, checking that he was OK and taking the driver's details – the driver did not have a licence! Then our colleague Margaret Swires rushed John (with Maria) off to the hospital where it was confirmed that nothing was broken.

Yes, it was a miracle, and even the police were amazed that John didn't end up like Humpty Dumpty!

At the Seminary, the administrative personnel were the same as was in place for the Leaders' Training Centre, at the time. These were Maria, who became the new Seminary's Administrative Coordinator, and Jeane Cleide, our office secretary. We continued to establish the working structure of the Seminary with the appointment of an Academic Coordinator, a Brazilian pastor-teacher with previous experience in theological education and a heart for the new project. A Librarian was also recruited, though we had few books to start with. By the time we had both left the Seminary in 2011, the Library boasted 3000 volumes and was considered to be the best and most up-to-date theological library in Natal. The purchase of books was made possible by generous donations from several charities in the United Kingdom and the separation of five percent of the Seminary's monthly receipts from student fees. There was also a monthly contribution from the state Baptist Convention.

We were answerable to the state Baptist Convention through a Junta that responded to the Convention for the work of the Seminary. There were two critical moments: firstly, when we decided the legal name of the Seminary, by which it was registered with the local education authority. There was opposition on the part of a few Junta members to the term 'School'

Natal Seminary Library

in the name, Baptist School for Ministerial Formation. They argued that the term 'School' would diminish the stature of the new Seminary. It was, however, to be used in a generic sense. The term was also used by Brazilian Theological Associations to denote their member institutions. This prejudice was not shared by all concerned, and the name was adopted.

Some years later, the Brazilian Ministry of Education determined that all theological seminaries in Brazil would have to adopt strict and expensive conditions, in order to use the term 'Seminary' in a legal sense. Fortunately, this was not a problem for us, as the

Potiguar Theological Seminary, as it was known by the churches, was legally registered as the Baptist School for Ministerial Formation, a term perfectly acceptable to the Brazilian education authorities.

The second critical moment came at a meeting of the Seminary Council. The Council dealt with matters of the curriculum and teaching practice within the Seminary. At one meeting at which I presided, I brought forward the subject of an entrance examination for new students. The test would have included knowledge of the Bible and General Knowledge. The Council decided not to adopt this measure, believing it would discourage prospective students from applying to the Seminary. I requested that it be recorded in the minutes of that meeting that I did not support the decision taken. Some years later, the students of our seminary were given the opportunity of doing a supplementary course from an institution whose courses were recognised by the Brazilian government. The successful completion of the additional course meant that the diplomas they had received from us were validated and recognised nationally. One of the requirements for the validation of diplomas was that students should have undertaken an entrance examination prior to starting their original course. It was ironic that one of the council members who voted against the proposal to have an entrance examination was the student representative on the Council.

In January 2005, less than 18 months after the Seminary had begun its existence, we wrote to our supporting churches in the United Kingdom:

So much is happening at the moment, and for all of it, we praise the Living God. The Seminary has blossomed and continues to be an exciting challenge. The development of courses and administrative structures keeps us on our toes. There seem to be an increasing number of meetings to discuss plans or report back, but this reflects the Seminary's onward march. We have a capable and dedicated group of teachers and office staff. It's great to be part of a team and see people grow together and as individuals.

The secret of running a successful seminary in Natal involved a delicate balancing act between income and expenditure. The cost to the students had to be viable for them to be able to do the course. Also, the number of students enrolled at any one time had to reach a pre-determined minimum number. The reality was that according to the income per capita of students, the Seminary required sixty students who were able to pay their way. This balance was achieved and maintained during the period of our service with the Seminary, not a penny less, not a penny more. This balancing act was another of God's miracles, seen in the outworking of our everyday practical affairs.

The time for the Seminary to be led by a Brazilian had arrived. One of my last acts as Director was described in our newsletter towards the end of 2009:

Baptist Seminary teaching session

In October, John travelled to Rio de Janeiro to the annual conference of the Association of Brazilian Baptist Theological Colleges, which gives recognition to seminaries in Brazil. He presented the credentials of our Seminary, and a unanimous decision was taken to grant us formal recognition. This was a great way to end our time at the Seminary and also to hand over to a Brazilian Director with this stamp of approval.

Serving the Mission and leading a church

During the time we lived in Natal, Maria served as BMS World Mission Administrator for Brazil. This involved financial aspects of BMS work and preparing the annual accounts. She was also responsible for sorting through the complex legal issues regarding the conclusion of BMS work in that country. We wrote about this in December 2009:

Maria has had a busy time with BMS administration in Brazil, as we deal with the closing down of the legal entity which is necessary for the mission to have a bank account and own properties in Brazil. This will bring the Brazil field into line with other countries where BMS work. As the number of mission personnel has diminished in Brazil over the past decade, so it has increased in countries such as Ecuador and Peru.

Between 2002 and 2006 we also had responsibility for the Living Water Baptist Church on the north side of Natal, the opposite side from where we lived. It is located in a poor district of the town on the road out to the new airport.

In December 2003, we sent the following update to our many friends and supporting churches back home:

The Living Water Baptist Congregation became a church in full standing in June and is going on well. Another baptism is being held on 7 December, John's birthday. We are also dealing with the legal documentation of the new church so that it officially exists in the sight of the authorities. Some of our most meaningful time, however, has been spent visiting homes and families around the church. It's proved an important way of identifying with the day to day lives of local people. One evening in November, we were at Ana's house when a neighbour arrived with her baby boy. He was born three months premature two months ago. He still weighed only 1.55 kilos. So tiny and fragile we prayed that little Luan would grow up to be strong and healthy and a loyal servant of Jesus Christ.

Our story is about other people's stories as well as our own. Often, the two are intricately woven together into a single fabric.

In August 2005, we wrote home:

We had a fantastic baptismal service on Pentecost Sunday (15 May), when John baptised the couple who he married two weeks previously. They confessed their faith in Christ together with their eldest son and two others – a lady (Jeania) and a girl of sixteen (Amanda). Please pray for Amanda whose life at home is difficult at the moment. Her father tore up her Bible, and she was away from church for a few weeks. We were really pleased that she came to the service last night, and the church has provided her with a new Bible to replace her old one.

The story of the couple mentioned in the paragraph above is an interesting one. They had lived happily together for about fourteen years; however, they were never officially married. To get married would have involved considerable financial costs. One day, they both asked for believers' baptism. This created a dilemma for the church. It was felt that they should not be baptised as they were living together, but not officially as a married couple. The church decided to pay their wedding costs. The marriage took place, and a beautiful and moving service it was. It was held in our tiny local Baptist church building. They were still very much in love, and that was clearly the main reason for their becoming 'husband and wife' in the eyes of the civil authorities. Two weeks later, they publically confessed their faith in our Lord Jesus Christ through the waters of baptism. The fact that their eldest son was also baptised on that occasion only added to the poignancy of the moment.

Worrying news from home

With our own teenage son living in England, you can imagine our thoughts were never far from him. When he became ill right in the middle of his GCSE AS-level exams, you can understand that we were concerned; being so far away from him in that situation, only added to our anxiety. That summer we shared our news with friends at home and how it affected Maria's own health:

In May, right in the middle of his AS level exams, JM went down with mumps. He was still able to do the exams, though he took most of them on his own in the sick bay. He had to push himself hard to get through all the work but had no complaints about the exam papers themselves. We are very grateful to the many of you who sent him e-mails, wishing him well. At the same time as JM was unwell, Maria went down with shingles, and those of you who may have had shingles will know how painful they can be.

Maria's shingles were most likely a direct result of worry and stress, which she was largely able to conceal and not let affect unduly her work in Brazil. She will always bear the physical scars of that worrying time, but our God is wonderfully present in all these situations. João Marcos took it all in his stride and achieved good grades that year. The following year he took his GCSE A levels and passed with precisely the grades required to do his chosen course at his preferred university.

Chapter Ten

Encore

In August 2008, BMS World Mission requested 'one last significant project' before my retirement. The agreed objective was to develop a lay leadership and ministerial training programme that could be used in the remotest corners of Brazil, where access to a course of theology was inaccessible both geographically and financially. As I left the Seminary in Natal for the last time as its Director, I remarked to one of our students that I would be remembered for the last thing I did. After thirty years of service in Brazil, we could have gone out with an excellent track record. We had no need of a further challenge to prove the point. This new challenge was uncharted territory; anything could happen.

To begin with, it was proposed by our BMS team leader that all the material be newly written and then made available to prospective students in printed book form. Well, it was a starting point. After considering the cost and logistics of using printed books, I decided a better approach would be to make the new material available through the Internet. As you will be aware, the Internet is the miracle communications tool of our age. The initial reaction was that very few people in the remotest parts of Brazil would have access to the Internet. This was a totally wrong assumption. Internet cafes had opened across Brazil and, for a small cost, access to the worldwide web was available to almost anyone with an interest in using it.

The Timothy Project, as the project was called, was launched in Brasilia (the Brazilian capital) on 19th January 2009. I presented the project, explaining its purpose and structure to a group of theological educators from all over Brazil. They responded positively to the new project and expressed the view that it would fill a gap in the area of leadership training in Brazil. A council of reference was appointed to give guidance to the project and serve as a sounding board as the project progressed. I was confirmed as Project Coordinator. The next step was to establish the kind of material that would be appropriate for our target audience. As our target market, we had in mind the riverside communities of the Amazon region. I had already met with the top brass of the Baptist denomination in Brazil. We had to then consult with the grassroots in our target area. To conduct this analysis, I travelled to the northeast state of Ceará.

I had set aside one day to meet with a group of Brazilian national missionaries. The meeting was at a Baptist church, high up in the mountains, two-hundred miles due west of the coastal city of Fortaleza, the state capital. These good people were serving national missionaries. I had met most of them on a previous teaching assignment in the state. We sat down together for a whole morning, and I listened to what they had to say.

The first eight modules to be produced were the direct result of the meeting with the missionaries. I had taken on board their suggestions for the course curriculum, and this was also in line with the needs of the local churches. Two years later, the material had been written and published on the Internet. Soon afterwards, requests to register began to flow in and in good numbers. In the month of January 2012 alone, we received forty applications to register with the Project. We continue today to receive requests from two new churches every week. The Timothy Project has received glowing tributes from churches in Brazil, Peru, Guinea-Bissau, Angola, Mexico and Guatemala, to name but a few.

Having decided the content of the material and how it was to be delivered to the students, it now needed to be designed. A young student from the Seminary in Natal, recently qualified as a teacher, was given the task of writing up some questions based on the first manual to be written. Not only did he do that, but he came up with a model for the teachers' manual, too. It was immediately adopted, and the outline has been used to this day for all of our teachers' manuals.

The importance of putting together a solid team was paramount. Several competent people were approached with a view to writing the student manuals. Almost all of these accepted the challenge and came up with the goods.

One other critical matter had to be resolved. What name should we give to the Project? Stuart Christine, our team leader, and I once discussed this on a long overnight bus journey. We threw out a few ideas but were none the wiser for our efforts. For several months I searched my mind for the elusive name. In the end, I settled on The Timothy Project. This title has a sound biblical basis, particularly in Paul's Second Letter to Timothy. In Chapter 2 and verse two, Paul exhorts Timothy to teach that which he had already learned from Paul to other capable persons, that they might teach others also. This encapsulates both the principles and the vision of the Project.

Beyond our dreams

Since then, the Project has exceeded our wildest dreams. It has grown, well beyond the remotest corners of Brazil, for which it was initially designed. It is now used widely in the Portuguese speaking world and has also been translated into Spanish and English. The total number of churches and organisations registered to receive the material currently exceeds one-thousand-two-hundred and represents thirty-five countries worldwide. The success has created its own problem.

BMS World Mission has always had a policy of supporting partner churches and organisations in the projects that they wished to develop. BMS provides the personnel required to either get these projects off the ground or to assist in their development. This is a good policy and is more likely to succeed than when a projectis imposed from outside. In the event of the Timothy Project, it has outgrown the scope of denominational organisations by evolving into an interdenominational project. It has also outgrown national church institutions by becoming an international project. A multi-lingual project also puts it beyond the scope of monolingual organisations. However, a solution may have been found, to which we shall return in a moment.

New modules have been prepared and uploaded to our website. The modules aim to show our students how to apply learning to the practical tasks of ministry. For this reason, the modules all follow the same basic principle, which is incorporated into their respective titles. All our modules begin with the words, 'How to.'

The following is a selection of Timothy Project titles:

'How to preach biblical messages';
'How to give the reason for your faith';
'How to grow in the spiritual life';
'How to speak of Jesus';
'How to care for creation';
'How to set up a social programme in your church';
'How to engage in mission'.

Timothy Project – Gethsemane Baptist Church, São Paulo

From small beginnings, the Timothy Project, and our ministry as a whole in Brazil has grown and grown. During one of our post-retirement visits to Brazil, we were contacted by BMS World Mission, in rural Oxfordshire. They asked if we knew how many churches had actually used the Timothy Project material. We already knew the number of registered churches, but not the number of those who had actually used the material as a tool for helping their members in the work of ministry.

Following this enquiry, a survey of churches enabled us to project that a third of registered churches have already used the Project to build the kingdom of God. About the same number are serious about using the material in the future.

The survey provided many insights into the evangelical church in Latin America and Africa, reflecting the vitality of the church on these continents. Brazil, in particular, is the most significant user, with the majority of our user churches coming from this dynamic centre of Christian mission. Three decades ago, social action was associated with Marxist ideology among Brazilian evangelical churches. Now, many of these are actively engaged in social action and are using the material the Timothy Project provides in this area of Christian outreach.

In addition to Brazil, churches from eleven other countries have used the Timothy Project manuals. These include Peru, Guatemala, Mexico, Guinea-Bissau, Angola, Mozambique and the United Kingdom.

From humble beginnings, leading a small congregation in the Amazon rainforest, God has blessed our ministry in wonderful ways. Initial misgivings about starting a new and very different project prior to our retirement have been completely dispelled. If the call and the initiative have come from God, then we need only to trust him to use our human efforts and to bless them, as Jesus blessed the fish and the loaves on Galilee's shores. The Timothy Project has more than a thousand students from nearly sixty churches. 21st-century communications technology enables us to do far more than was possible when we first went to Brazil.

To paraphrase the apostle Paul: 'To one is given the task of planting, and to another the task of watering, but it is God who gives the increase' (1 Corinthians 3.6). How this has proved true throughout our years of service in Brazil. We are called to bear fruit that lasts. The fruit produced is a legitimate testimony to our work for the Lord. There is great joy in seeing others to whom we have given a helping hand, going on with the Lord. They have born even more fruit than we could possibly have grown on our own.

The challenge was always to build on previous experience, but also to venture further than we had gone before. Frequently, we seemed to be stepping beyond the familiar and living outside of our comfort zone, until we felt comfortable again. That was always a sign that it was time to move on; to take up a new and different challenge; to put at risk the acclaim for previous gains and achievements.

An exciting development regarding the future of the Timothy Project involves a mission-minded church on the East Kent coast. This quintessential English town church is providing a permanent home for the Project, and is perhaps the final link in the chain, ensuring the long-term future of the Timothy Project, which continues to receive requests from churches around the world, eager to receive the material we produce. I say 'perhaps the last link in the chain,' because one never knows what God might do next. He is a God of surprises, but his purpose is always to bless us and, through us, to extend his kingdom from shore to shore. At the time of writing, a church organisation from Honduras has registered. This is the first request from a church or organisation in that country. We move on in faith that God who has brought us this far, will lead us to tomorrow's opportunities. We have come a long way since we started out in Brazil nearly forty years ago. The number forty is a significant number in the Bible. It occurs many times and has a symbolic as well as literal meaning. It means a sufficient period of time and is used in association with significant events in history. For example, the forty days and nights that rain fell on the earth in the days of Noah; the forty years of Israel's wanderings in the desert; the forty days that Jesus was in the Judean desert, following his baptism in the river Jordan; the forty days between his resurrection and ascension to heaven. So, the fortieth anniversary of our arriving in Brazil is a significant moment. For the years that God has given us, we praise him. For the years that remain, we look to him.

Chapter Eleven

The times we've lived through

Maria and I lived in Brazil through times of significant economic and political upheaval in Brazil. In the late 1970s, the military regime was beginning to open the door to the return of democratic rule. This was known as *abertura*. The process began during the government of General Ernesto Geisel and was taken forward by his successor, General João Figueiredo. Democracy was partially restored in January 1985, though only two parties were allowed to participate in the election of the new president. These were the Government's party, ARENA, the Alliance for National Renewal, and the PMDB, the Brazilian Democratic Movement Party. The Government put forward Paulo Maluf as their candidate, a seasoned politician from São Paulo. The other was Tancredo Neves, the people's candidate, who also enjoyed the respect of João Figueiredo. These elections did not represent full-blown democracy. The people did not cast a single vote, only the politicians who were part of the military government, none of whom had been elected by the people.

The evening before his inauguration, Tancredo Neves was taken ill while attending Mass in Brasilia, the nation's capital. Conspiracy theories abounded, but these were never substantiated. Tancredo underwent numerous operations, but after each one deteriorated further. He died five weeks later and the vice-president elect, José Sarney, took office. Sarney had defected from the Government party before the elections and was considered a traitor by Figueiredo. Such was Figueiredo's displeasure at the whole turn of events that he refused to take part in the handing over ceremony. It was customary for the outgoing president to pass the sash of office to his successor, but this significant moment did not materialise. The outgoing president, João Figueiredo, refused to attend and perform this final duty of office. Democracy in Brazil had got off to an inauspicious start.

José Sarney was a landowner from the backwater state of Maranhão. He was a poet and an eloquent speaker. During the run-up to the presidential election, he had defected from the ARENA party to the newly formed PMDB, perhaps out of political expediency. It was for this reason that João Figueiredo refused to hand over to Sarney the presidential sash. In his first television broadcast, President Sarney declared that destiny had placed him in office. This could not detract from one important fact: Sarney had not won the hearts of the people as Tancredo Neves had done before him. He did, however, represent the people's aspiration for a return to full democracy at the next presidential election.

In the course of time, the people's aspiration for a new political system was to turn into Brazil's nightmare, and in spectacular fashion. In January

1990, Fernando Collor de Mello was inaugurated as president of Brazil by popular vote. He was young and confident and started out by projecting a youthful, energetic image. He was a breath of fresh air in the early days, but this was soon to change. He changed his appearance to project a more serious image. He darkened his hair and greased it so that it lost its youthfulness. In order to bring down inflation, he encouraged the population to *pechinchar* or haggle over the price of things in the shops. We thought he was on our side, but we were mistaken. One evening, on the six o'clock news, came the astonishing announcement that all savings accounts had been frozen. The idea was to reduce spending and bring down inflation. The problem was that these savings accounts, known as *poupança,* were the savings of ordinary Brazilians. These accounts paid interest and were used like current accounts to pay utility bills and provide for the family. Overnight Fernando Collar had turned the people against him. Some concessions were made to the most vulnerable, such as widows on small pensions, to access their funds. Even so, Brazil was in a state of turmoil. The President was also being accused of corruption, which he vehemently denied. He was still confident that he had the support of the people and invoked a protest march in support of his presidency. The people turned out in their masses, but to Collar's surprise and dismay they were calling for his resignation.

Impeachment charges were brought against him in Congress. He fought these charges to the end, but on the eve of an impeachment vote, on 29th December 1992, knowing that his fate was decided, he resigned. Even so, he was banned from politics for eight years. Today he is back as a senator; such is the way of Brazilian politics.

The so-called 'Economic Miracle', which characterised the late sixties to the late seventies, was based on massive government borrowing at low interest rates. Vast sums of money were borrowed by the military government from the World Bank and the International Monetary Fund. With the rise in interest rates in the years following military rule, the country was in the position of paying back vast amounts in interest, but making few inroads into the capital sums initially borrowed. The situation reached the point where the Brazilian government refused to continue servicing a debt which it had no hope of ever repaying.

By the early 1990s, the Brazilian currency had become virtually worthless. It had been devalued by the Brazilian Government a thousand-fold on three occasions in the troubled times following the economic miracle. The currency also changed name from the Cruzeiro to the Cruzado, to the Cruzado Novo and back to the Cruzeiro, between 1978 and 1994. In the months before the introduction of the Real, on 1st July 1994, prices in the shops were linked to the US Dollar. The price of goods, from groceries to ballpoint pens, was increasing on a daily basis according to the rate of exchange. It was impossible to budget for household expenses, let alone for a business.

One morning, in June 1994, I overheard a conversation in a small cafe on my way to our extension course in Taquaral. The owner of the cafe was talking to a sales representative and asked him about the price he would have to pay for his next order in a week's time. The answer was that prices would inevitably go up again, even within the space of a week. I must confess to feeling a strong sense of resentment at this state of affairs. I felt that commercial traders were taking advantage of the situation, at the expense of the already hard up average Brazilian. Fortunately, this economic turmoil was only to last a few more weeks. With the introduction of the Real, the economy was turned around. In fact, the Real was initially worth slightly more than the Dollar and maintained parity for almost two years.

The years 1992-1994 saw the restoration of political stability under Itamar Franco, who as Collor's vice-president, assumed office in his place. It was at the close of Franco's presidency that the Real was introduced, although the Finance minister, Fernando Henrique Cardoso, took most of the credit for this. FHC, as he was affectionately known, is a sociologist and an intellectual. He easily won in the presidential elections in October 1994. During his mandate, he restored respectability to Brazilian politics as well as the economy. He was elected to a second term of office in 1998 and was considered to be a safe pair of hands. FHC's primary opponent on the two occasions he ran for office was Luiz Inácio Lula da Silva, a former trade union leader from the Workers' Party. Lula was finally successful at the third attempt when FHC was ineligible to contest the election. The Brazilian political scene had changed dramatically since the days of military rule.

Many Brazilians were fearful of the direction in which Lula would take the country. To my surprise, he kept the economy on track and was the most popular Brazilian president of all time. Though Lula did not speak English or any other foreign language, he was widely admired and respected overseas. It was not until he left office in 2011, after fulfilling two consecutive mandates that his political world began to unravel. Widespread corruption was discovered in the state-owned petroleum company Petrobras. Bribes on a colossal scale had been paid to politicians by businesses for securing contracts with Petrobras. Lula was tried and given a prison sentence but has been allowed to remain free while he appeals against his conviction.

Lula's chosen successor, Dilma Rousseff, completed one term of office and won a second term by a slim majority of votes. Despite her victory at the polls, her first term did not end on a high note. In particular, her handling of the economy was heavily criticised.

Early in her second term of office accusations were brought against her for falsifying the Federal accounts at the end of her previous mandate. Accounting methods were used to hide the real facts behind the Brazilian economy. Though she admitted to using so-called creative accounting methods designed to conceal the facts, she claimed to have done only what other governments had done before. Rousseff's situation was further complicated insofar as she was President of Petrobras during the period of the corruption scandal. Although there was no proof that she was directly involved in any wrongdoing, she was suspected of knowing what was going on. And if she didn't know, it was argued she should have done. Both houses of Congress found her guilty of manipulating the Federal accounts, and she was impeached and removed from office on 31st August 2016. Democracy has not been a complete success story in Brazil. Even when the people have the right to elect their leaders, they do not always get what they want. Democracy does have its limitations, but for those Brazilians who lived through twenty-one years of military rule, democracy is far better.

Two of Brazil's civilian presidents suffered persecution under the military. The quest to expunge the country of communists meant exile for Fernando Henrique Cardoso and torture and prison for Dilma Rousseff. This was only the tip of the iceberg, as hundreds more disappeared and were never seen again. To make matters worse, neighbour would take revenge against neighbour with the accusation of being a communist, if there had been a quarrel or disagreement between them.

Violence, aggression and God's protection

In present-day Brazil, it would seem that the military has no appetite or desire to rule again. However, some look back with nostalgia to those days when law and order prevailed. Today the streets are more violent and people less safe. I know of several friends who have been assaulted either waiting for a bus, on the bus or getting off the bus in Natal.

During a meeting at church, Maria and the group she was with were held at gunpoint, and our car was taken. It was later found not far from the prison, probably to be used to assist in an escape from that institution. As a family, we were held at gunpoint in our own home. The assailants took the opportunity of getting in as Maria was returning from the shops. One of the two assailants went inside the house and told us to go with him. The other took the house keys and tried to lock the front gate. He took his time, and his junior partner stepped outside the side door to see why he was taking so long. With just a hair's breadth between the assailant and the door, I slammed the door behind him and locked it. We moved further into the house and locked another door on the way, which could only be locked and unlocked from the inside. We called the police and informed the pastor of our church. When they arrived, the assailants had disappeared, leaving the house keys by the front gate. A situation like that could have had a very different outcome. I believe that an angel of the Lord stood between our assailants and ourselves. We didn't see that angel, but our assailants did. Whatever happened, something caused them to change their minds and flee the scene.

A story is told by Billy Graham of a Christian family in China at the time of the Communist Revolution. Soldiers were sent to arrest the family at their home. As they approached the house they suddenly stopped; then retreated. Afterwards one of the soldiers explained that they had seen heavenly beings with flaming swords standing in front of the house. The family were unaware of the presence of these angels, but the soldiers saw them very clearly. And because of the presence of these angels, the Chinese soldiers desisted in their mission. I believe we were similarly protected as a family on that early evening in June 2006.

Brazil is a fantastically beautiful country, yet it is marred and flawed by violence on the streets and corruption in politics. We have, however, been privileged to serve God in that country for thirty-three years, and he has been faithful to us through all that time. We have heard about God's faithfulness through the testimony of the Bible and his servants of old. Now we have seen it with our own eyes and proved it in our own experience. God is our trustworthy defender in times of danger, and he can be yours, too. Because God is unseen does not mean he is absent or does not exist. His presence is not necessarily accessible to our five physical senses, but we can be made aware of his presence by our spiritual sense, which is just as real.

Chapter Twelve

A final twist of events

This brief account of our life and work in Brazil must draw to a close. God has been good, very good, and has been there for us all the way and in every situation. If we could begin over again, we would do the same. Maybe, with hindsight, some things would be done differently. That will always be true. We cannot know the results of our endeavours until after the event. That is in the very nature of things. But that does not stop us going forward a day at a time, taking risks for the cause we serve. God, himself, took the risk of sending his only Son into the world. To love is to take a risk. God has taken the risk of loving us. We are creatures of free choice and can respond in different ways to his love, made known on the Cross. When we give of ourselves to others we are taking a risk; the risk of being accepted or rejected. We have no rights, other than to God's guidance and protection when we step out in his name. The course of events was not always smooth or trouble free. Even at the end of our service in Brazil, there was a significant problem.

We had travelled to the United Kingdom in June 2010 for my mother-in-law's ninetieth birthday, and also for our son's graduation from the University of Manchester, which took place the following month. Soon after our arrival, I began to experience severe abdominal pain. One afternoon the pain became so severe, I went to A & E at the Queen Elizabeth the

Queen Mother Hospital in Margate. I was checked over, given medication and then sent home. A couple of days later the pain returned, and I was back at A & E. I was again checked over and given morphine to relieve the pain. This time, however, the doctor who attended me decided to admit me to the hospital for further tests.

Initial tests and scans were inconclusive. So, I was sent for an MRI scan, which would give a much clearer picture of what was wrong. This scan showed that I had a small gallstone lodged in the common bile duct. The hospital did not have a slot for the necessary endoscopic procedure that day. The following day, I was due to travel to Manchester for our son's graduation ceremony. The doctor reluctantly allowed me to leave the hospital and to make the journey but gave me a date for the procedure the day after I returned home.

The journey to Manchester was most distressing, as I suffered severe pain and was unable to do any of the driving on the outward journey. Maria and her mother were also with me in the car on that long and challenging drive. I was only able to eat soups and the like but miraculously was in no pain during the whole of the graduation ceremony. On our journey home, the pain returned, and I was glad to arrive at the hospital the following day for the endoscopic procedure to remove the offending gallstone. The procedure was carried out swiftly and successfully in the outpatient's department of the hospital.

While I was an in-patient earlier in the week, the doctors discovered that there was a problem with my colon. How this was detected was a miracle. I had been in considerable pain one afternoon from the gallstone and had just taken some medication. As I was waiting for this to take effect, I began walking along the hospital corridor outside the ward. Returning to the ward, I met the consultant surgeon who was responsible for my care, in the corridor. He was talking with one of his team and asked me how I was feeling. I explained to him the pain I had been suffering that afternoon, but that the medication was, by then, taking effect.

The following morning, when he was doing his hospital rounds, he came to see me in the usual way. He said that as a result of our conversation the previous afternoon, he had shown my scans to the senior radiologist. It was then that the alteration in my colon was detected and an appointment made for a colonoscopy. The result was given to me by the MacMillan nurse. It was cancer.

I was booked in for surgery on 20th September 2010. The procedure involved the removal of half my colon, but also fourteen lymph nodes. The histology report confirmed that two of the removed lymph nodes were cancerous. The cancer had spread outside my colon and was already at the third stage of its progression. Fortunately, it had not spread to my liver or lungs. I was prescribed a programme of chemotherapy. The chemo was to 'mop up' any rogue cells that might still be in my bloodstream. I was told that these could not be detected by even the most advanced scans. The chemotherapy was, therefore, a precaution, and was given to reduce the risk of the cancer returning. Alarms bells rang almost continuously during my treatment, as blood tests strongly indicated a recurrence of the disease. Fortunately, further procedures did not confirm a recurrence, and I continued with the treatment. A month before the treatment was due to end, my blood test results began to turn slowly in the right direction. The consensus was that some rogue cancer cells had been present and that as the chemotherapy was killing these, so a substance was secreted into my bloodstream, the same substance as happens with live cancer cells.

This story is remarkable for another reason. The afternoon I met the consultant surgeon on the hospital corridor, I had been offered medication at two o'clock, shortly before visiting hours. As I was not in any pain at the time, I declined this medication, not wishing to take painkillers unnecessarily. Towards the end of visiting, the pain began to return. After my visitors had left, I asked the nursing sister if I could have something to relieve the pain, which she said she would give me. In fact, the medication was not brought until the routine distribution of medication at five-thirty. So shortly before six, I was still in some discomfort and began my walk along the hospital corridor.

Walking seemed to help to relieve the pain. If I had been given the painkillers an hour earlier, I would not have been walking in the hospital corridor and would not have met the consultant surgeon. If I had not met the consultant surgeon, our conversation would not have taken place. If that meeting had not taken place, he would not have shown my scans to the senior radiologist. If the senior radiologist had not seen my scans, the cancer would not have been detected and it would have spread further. If it had spread further, I would not be writing this book today.

A lasting testimony

I was fit enough to return to Brazil in August 2011. In effect, we had lost the whole of our final period of service in Brazil. We packed up our belongings, handed over our rented house and moved south to Curitiba where we had a property of our own. The BMS kindly allowed an extension to our service, to enable us to attend the annual assembly of the Brazilian Baptist Convention, where we received a beautifully inscribed plaque in recognition of our long service in Brazil.

God's people are not exempt from illness and the disruption to life and work that this can bring. Though I lost the final year of missionary service in Brazil, I was able to continue working at the Timothy Project. The online nature of the Project meant that I was able to continue with my work in the United Kingdom as if I had been in Brazil.

As we look back over the years, we can see God's hand upon us at every turn, in our lives as well as in our ministry. We have experienced the joy of seeing people enter full-time Christian ministry in the United Kingdom and Brazil from churches we have led or been involved with, from the early days in Birmingham to our last posting in Natal. In addition, many others have gone on to serve their churches; better equipped than before we knew them. On the other hand, we have also experienced thorns in the flesh in the churches and institutions we have served. These may have been allowed to keep us dependent on the Lord, just as with the apostle Paul. The thorns, however, were also a distraction from the work we had been called to do.

Looking back, on two occasions these thorns in the flesh were caused by individuals who were ambitious to take over from us, but lacked the patience to wait for the right moment. A few

problematic occasions were when the devil used people (always insiders) to derail the church through cunning and deceit. Well, of course, that is in the very nature of the devil's work. Our response was to identify the problem, isolate it, and then deal with the cause. In every such case, the

Farewell to Brazil

church united behind its leader and dealt effectively with the problem. At these times, the church has to make a stand for what it believes to be right. Neutrality in such matters never wins the day.

Our aim in Brazil was always to work ourselves out of a job. That is in the very nub of missionary work. While doing the job, we are always in the process of training others to take over from us. This is known as mentoring. The first phase of mentoring is to do the job while others observe your work; the second step is to allow others to do the job while you observe them doing the job; the third stage is to allow them to do the job on their own, while you move on to something else. We have always tried to operate in this way in Brazil. After all, the real test of ministry is what you leave behind. If you leave the church in a worse state than you found it, then your contribution to its life will have been negative. If you leave the church as you found it, then you will have achieved nothing at all, for good or bad. If you leave the church stronger and better equipped to engage in God's mission, then you will have done well. It's worth repeating that the real and definitive test of our work is the long-term effect it has on the church and the kingdom of God. Jesus commanded us to go and bear fruit; fruit that lasts long after we have left the scene. It is what we leave behind, not what we take with us that counts.

It is the custom of Brazilian Baptists to present a plaque as a token of their recognition of the work of missionaries who have served in their country. This recognition is given in various forms but is often done in the name of the state Baptist Convention, since it is at this level that we have a relationship with the local churches. Often gifts of other kinds are given by the local churches and organisations. Some awards are given as formal recognition of our work; others are more spontaneous. One of these was presented by the students of our extension course in Antonina. It is a beautiful wood carving of some brightly painted houses in this colonial town. The idea behind the gift was that we should also remember them, as they remember us. Another gift was really quite unexpected. The gift was associating the Seminary library with my name, an initiative of my successor as Director of the Seminary. Although the library, boasting 3000 volumes, and the most up-to-date theological library in the state, was assembled during our watch, we were greatly moved by this act of affection and generosity. The final act of recognition was given at the Annual Assembly of the Brazilian Baptist Convention when we were called to the front and speeches made about our thirty-three years of service in Brazil. Another plaque was presented graciously alluding to our 'notable missionary work' and 'fruitful ministry' in the country as a whole.

Andrew White, an Anglican missionary to the Middle East, has faced many challenges during the course of his travels and ministry of reconciliation. In a recent account of his experiences, he called the congregation not to take care, but to take risks. Every day we have to choose the level of risk we are prepared to accept. Getting out of bed in the morning is a risk, but we do get out of bed in the morning. Then having got out of bed, we decide what we are going to do with our day. The really big question, though, isn't about what we are going to do with our day, but at the end of the day, how have we used it? How have we used that precious and unique time that we will never have again? And even more, significant questions will inevitably arise as the years go by: How have we used the time God has given us? How have we used our lives in this world and for this world? The greatest source of inner peace and well-being is to be able to look back with gratitude for all he has chosen to do in our lives; also for those people he has brought into our lives, and who have enriched us beyond measure.

One day, I was sitting having lunch with an American missionary, who had come to a pastors' retreat I had organised at the Baptist Camp in Santa Catarina. He had travelled by car from Curitiba with Dr Roberto Silvado, the senior pastor of the Bacacheri Baptist Church, the second largest in the state of Paraná. Dr Silvado was also on the speaking team for our retreat and had come to talk about leadership. He is currently President of the Brazilian Baptist Convention, a man well respected among Baptists in Brazil and in the United States, where he studied for his doctorate. As we were talking, the American missionary shared with me his conversation with Dr

Silvado on the five-hour journey from Curitiba. I refer to this because it is how I should like our relationship with the Brazilian people to be remembered.

The American missionary looked at me and said: 'Roberto was saying on the journey here that John has the heart of a Brazilian.' This is, to my mind, the simplest, purest expression of what it means to be a missionary. That these words came not from a British or an American missionary, but a Brazilian pastor, is why I would choose them as the definitive testimony to our work in Brazil. To the ordinary people of Brazil, Maria was more Brazilian than me, especially since she speaks Portuguese without a trace of an accent. Her part Latin blood also gives her the appearance of a Brazilian, as does her name. So, I share this tribute wholeheartedly and unreservedly with her.

Our magnificent prayer warriors

We cannot leave out of our story the many churches and friends in Scotland, Wales and England, who have supported us in prayer and encouraged us with their letters over three decades. Without these loyal 'rope holders' our mission would have been impossible. But the impossible became possible because these wonderful people were committed to world mission as much as us. Their unstinted financial giving through BMS World Mission freed us from material concerns. As such, we were able to focus entirely on our work and engage in all the tasks and challenges before us. We cannot measure the significance of their contribution, and will only know in heaven the magnitude of difference it made to our work.

From the smallest beginnings, great things can be achieved. Like the mustard seed to which Jesus referred in one of his parables. For our part, into the bargain, God has kept us safe when danger was close at hand. He has guided us when we ventured into uncharted waters. He has given us courage to go on when life was hardest. He has brought us through every situation to a more expansive place. He has blessed us as a family with an incalculable, enduring return for our investment.

The splendour of the heavens

Now to our final story: it was 3rd November 1994, and we had been living in Santa Catarina for just over a year. South America was to experience a solar eclipse. The path of totality was to pass south of Brusque where we lived, so we left home at eight in the morning and travelled south for three hours. We had got as far as the coastal town of Rincão. The moon had already taken a large bite out of the sun. As we were near the sea, we decided to turn off the main road and head for the beach. We had never been to this spot before. The beach was quite deserted and unspoilt. A short while after we arrived, a small group of people came along. There were already a few photographers nearby with cameras mounted on sturdy tripods.

Then came the moment we had been waiting for and the sight we had come to see. There are no words to adequately describe what we experienced that morning. The air cooled dramatically, and there was an eeriness all around. Day turned to night, and the stars came out. I even spotted one of the planets close to the sun. The most marvellous thing for me was the blazing corona of the sun shining all around the black disk of the moon. Maria came prepared with a strip of film negative. The sun was completely covered by the moon for a full four minutes. There was time to share our film negative with the few people around us. Maria offered this to one girl in her teens, but the girl had turned away from the sun and, for fear, could not bring herself to witness this spectacle of nature. It was, whichever way one looked, an unforgettable moment. Even so, the brightness of the sun will be more perfectly eclipsed, when the creator of heaven and earth comes on the clouds with his angels.

This is our story. His alone is the glory.

Index of stories